D0406747

201 GAMES for the ELEMENTARY PHYSICAL EDUCATION PROGRAM

Jerry D. Poppen

PARKER PUBLISHING COMPANY

Library of Congress Cataloging-in Publication Data

Poppen, Jerry D.
  201 games for the elementary physical education program / Jerry D. Poppen.
      p. cm
  Includes index.
  ISBN 0-13-042061-1
    1. Physical education and training—Study and teaching (Elementary)   2. Games. I.
  Title: Two hundred one games for the elementary physical education program.   II. Title:
  Two hundred and one games for the elementary physical elementary education program.
  III. Title.

GV361.P56   2002
372.86′044—dc21

                                                                      2001036687

Printed in the United States of America

10 9 8 7 6 5 4 3 2 1

ISBN 0-13-042061-1

PARKER PUBLISHING COMPANY
Paramus, NJ 07652

DEDICATION

This book is dedicated to my grandchildren, David, Rachel, Rowan, and Catherine, who I hope have the opportunity to participate in a "Success Oriented Physical Education" program and learn to appreciate and understand the need to be physically fit for a lifetime.

ACKNOWLEDGMENTS

Because these games have been collected over the past 38 years, it is impossible to give specific credit for games that were shared at workshops and conventions by colleagues. I do, however, wish to thank all the colleagues whom I have learned from and shared with over the years.

ABOUT THE AUTHOR

Jerry Poppen's 38-year career in physical education has been spent in the Washington State Public Schools and as a part-time physical education instructor at Pacific Lutheran University in Tacoma, Washington. He has successfully used all of the games in *201 Games for the Elementary Physical Education Program* with elementary students in his elementary physical education programs. He has also taught the success-oriented philosophy on which this book is based in elementary physical education methods courses at the university level.

In workshops and seminars across the United States, Jerry Poppen shares his physical education philosophy of increasing player participation through "Success Oriented Physical Education."

Jerry practices what he preaches and leads a very active life that includes plenty of racquetball and bicycle riding. He is the author of four successful physical education books and continues to develop physical education resource materials to assist classroom teachers, physical educators, and recreation leaders. He believes that now more than ever—as hi-tech entertainment replaces physical activity in children's lives—that the importance of physical fitness and the joy of movement needs to be instilled in our American youth as well as in people of all ages.

ABOUT THIS BOOK

According to *Webster's New Compact Dictionary*, a game is defined as a diversion, a contest for amusement, or a scheme or plan of action. Other definitions indicate that a game is a competitive activity between two or more people, governed by rules to determine superiority. One author, Terry Orlick, believes that games can also be played on a cooperative, rather than competitive, basis. For a game to be cooperative, Mr. Orlick says that it must involve teamwork, acceptance of all participants, and involvement by all participants.

The collection of games in this book runs the gamut of the above definitions. You will find both competitive and cooperative activities, and activities that challenge the participants to develop a scheme or plan of action in order to achieve success. All the games included in this book are designed to maximize participation and minimize failure for all participants.

For games to be effective tools in the physical education program, they must be played to accomplish specific learning objectives and be part of a broad-based physical education program that allows students to develop varied and complementary skills.

For a game to make a contribution to a broad-based program, it needs to fulfill either a stated or implied educational purpose. While games are normally accepted as activities for enjoyment and teamwork, almost every game has an inherent learning objective. This book was written to assist you in selecting appropriate games to use in conjunction with specific educational purposes. And because the games are categorized according to their strategy and developmental levels, your selection of the right games for your teaching goals will be easier.

There are thousands of games in our world. Those you will find in *201 Games for the Elementary Physical Education Program* include a variety of games that were found to be very successful with elementary children. Some are old standbys, others were discovered at workshops and conferences, and others yet were originated by me. In several instances, you will find that I have modified a particular game to make it more applicable to elementary age children. I have also included proven teaching strategies for making these activities meaningful. The games are basically oriented toward use in physical education classes, but recreational leaders, camp counselors, youth group advisors, and anyone else who works with elementary school age youngsters will find this book a useful guide in presenting games that children will enjoy.

CONTENTS

		PLAY AREA		
GAME	**Grade Level**	**Gym**	**Grass**	**Playground**
Section 1. Movement Awareness Games 1				
1. No Touch	K–6	X	A	A
2. Statues	1–6	X		
3. High Fives	2–6	X	X	
4. Shadowing	3–6	X		
5. Living Letters	1–4	X		
6. Daytona Speedway	1–6	X	X	
7. Motorcycle Race	2–6	X	X	
8. Stock Car Race	2–6	X	X	
9. Bumper Cars	2–6	X	X	
10. Big Mack Truck Race	3–6	X	X	
Section 2. Circle Games 13				
11. Objectelephantitus	K–2	X		
12. Color Mix	K–1	X		
13. Mousetrap	K–1	X	X	
14. Spaceship	K–2	X	X	
15. Horse and Jockey	2–6	X		
16. Circle Chase	3–6	X	X	X
17. Shoe Pass	3–6	X		
Section 3. Single Line Games 23				
18. Octopus	K–2	X	X	X
19. Midnight	K–2	X	X	X
20. The Three Bears	K–2	X	X	X
21. Little Brown Bear	K–2	X	X	X
22. Martians	K–2	X	X	X
23. Black Bear	1–3	X	X	X
24. Spiders and Flies	1–3	X	X	X
25. Across the Great Divide	2–5	X	X	X
26. White Bear	1–3	X	X	X

Section 9. GAMES INVOLVING STRIKING SKILLS AND EYE-HAND COORDINATION 177

USING GAMES SUCCESSFULLY IN YOUR PHYSICAL EDUCATION PROGRAM

The intention of this book is to provide you with a large selection of games that you can use, not just to get students excited about playing, but to help them develop specific physical education skills. And in keeping with the motto "All active, all successful," the games featured in this book are designed for maximum involvement by all players.

The instructions for each game are self-explanatory and include a brief introduction; an equipment list; game preparation guidelines, which in some cases also include a diagram; and game play instructions. Many of the games also include tips for varying the game to keep it fresh or modifying the game to accommodate your students' ability levels. Many games are suitable for all elementary grade levels; however, recommended grade levels are provided for each game.

ENSURING PLAYERS' SAFETY

When it comes to safety in the gym, apparatus work or gymnastics get a lot of attention, and so do team sports that involve a lot of running and physical contact. But what about safety in line or tag games? Teachers may take safety for granted in these games, in part because children often play them on their own and no equipment is involved. However, children do need to be taught how to play games safely just as they are taught to participate in gymnastics and team sports safely.

The following guidelines will help you reduce accidents and injuries in your physical education program:

- Help children master spatial awareness before moving on to more advanced team games and reinforce spatial awareness skills on an ongoing basis.

- Teach students to stop and start on given signals.

- Keep the indoor play area free of obstacles and make sure floors are completely dry.

- Ensure that the outdoor play area is free of holes, debris, posts, or other obstacles that could cause children to trip.

- Establish boundaries and lines at least 8 to 10 feet away from walls and fences so children will not run into them.

- Teach children how to use any special equipment before using it in a game.

- Require that students dress safely. Children may be bare-foot or wear athletic shoes indoors; outdoors, athletic shoes should always be worn. Jewelry such as chains, dangling earrings, or protruding rings are an unnecessary hazard.

ACHIEVING A LEARNING OBJECTIVE

Games offer students an opportunity to apply the movement skills they have learned in a competitive or cooperative situation. To make games an integral part of your physical education program as well as a rewarding experience for every student, consider the following questions:

- Is the game being played for a purpose?

- Is the game appropriate for the emotional and physical maturity level of the students?

- Is there potential for students to be embarrassed through peer pressure?

- Does the game teach motor skills?

- Are all students receiving maximum playing time?

- Will every student have a feeling of success at the end of the game?

- Can the game be played without putting children at risk of being injured?

(These questions are based on material taken from Neil F. Williams' *The Physical Education Hall of Shame*. JOPHERD. August, 1992.) When choosing games for your physical education program, first define the learning objective you want to achieve. There is an endless list of specific instructional objectives that an effective physical educator can accomplish through games. The most common are:

- Improving fundamental movement abilities in locomotor, non-locomotor, and manipulative skills

- Enhancing the use of spatial awareness skills by learning to move safely within marked boundaries

- Applying the skill of changing directions for the purpose of avoiding contact with others; dodging and feinting; guarding a space, an object, or other players

- Learning to stop quickly and effectively

- Changing speeds smoothly and efficiently while moving in general space

- Improving aerobic endurance, flexibility, and strength

- Improving speed, agility, and coordination

- Promoting positive social interaction for the purpose of developing group spirit, group cooperation, sportsmanship, competition, positive self-image

- Promoting readiness skills such as listening and following directions and thinking strategically

By using games for a purpose, you can allow students a sense of accomplishment in having acquired new skills and used them to advantage in a competitive or cooperative game situation. In addition, over time students will develop a better understanding of how to apply each skill in different situations.

ENHANCING PLAYERS' EXPERIENCE

Once you have chosen a game that meets your desired instructional objective, it is time to present it to the children. A good technique is to use the learning principle referred to as the "anticipatory set" to introduce new activities. This is a way of helping students understand an upcoming event or activity by relating it to something they have already experienced in their lives. For example, to teach children a particular tag game, you can use a discussion of a real-life adventure that relates to the activity and discuss the particular skill they will learn from the game. Follow this by sharing with students the objective of the game they are playing. This will help them understand the rules of the game more thoroughly and increases their enthusiasm for the game. In addition to using the anticipatory set, the following instructional procedures will enhance your presentation of the game.

- Have the class under control.

- Know the game well before teaching it.

- Whenever possible, have players take their positions in the starting formation before explaining the rules.

- Establish boundaries and identify safety hazards.

- Present rules sequentially. When possible, combine the oral explanation with a demonstration.

- Be brief and to the point. If the game has several rules, get started and fill in the needed rules as the situations arise.

There are also steps you can take to keep the game experience as positive and problem-free as possible. The following guidelines are a good starting point:

- Use identification equipment, such as vests, pinnies, or armbands, to distinguish between teams or groups.

- Before beginning the game, ensure that students have sufficient understanding of the rules, or conduct a trial play period before playing a full-length game.

- While play is under way, guide the children by reinforcing the lesson objectives and raising questions to stimulate thinking by the students.

- Monitor players for fatigue.

- Do not allow players to scream or yell excessively, or to behave in an unduly rough manner.

- Stress enjoyment, not competition.

- Be alert. End the game before it fizzles out.

After playing the game, a well-planned closure or oral evaluation will tell you if the specific objective was met or if students understood the game. Use a question-and-answer session, not a lecture, to evaluate understanding. (You can find further information on teaching an objective, the use of active participation, and closures in Dr. Madeline Hunter's material on "Instructional Theory into Practice.")

MAXIMIZING PARTICIPATION

The current focus in quality physical education is success-oriented—meaning that every player should feel positive about his or her contribution to the game, regardless of whether the player (or his or her team) won the competition. To create this type of physical education environment, you must provide games and activities that maximize participation and minimize the risk of failure for all players.

A student cannot benefit from a game unless he or she is actively involved. Because it is nearly impossible to have all students active all the time, a minimum standard to strive toward is to have 50 percent of the students active 80 percent of the time. This sounds easier than it is. For example, in a game of kickball, half the players are on the offensive team, meaning they are sitting around waiting for their turn to kick. And what about the defensive players? Just because they are out in the field does that mean they are actively participating? I do not recommend this type of team game unless you can make some necessary modifications to speed it up and give more children more opportunities to catch, throw, and kick.

Relays are another type of game that must be carefully evaluated. Many times, we feel that because we have all of the children on a team, they are involved in the activity. But that's not necessarily the case. In a simple relay with five players on a team, each player is active just one-fifth of the time. If each student's turn to perform a task takes twenty seconds, each student is active only twenty out of the total one-hundred seconds that the relay might last. This clearly falls short of the goal of 50 percent active 80 percent of the time.

There are many games that are old-standbys and staples of many physical education (or recreational) programs that you should carefully evaluate before incorporating into your own program. These include:

- Circle games such as *Duck Duck Goose*. Two people are active at a time, the goose is set up for failure, and often, friends pick friends to be the next goose. Clearly, participation in this game is limited.

- Dodge ball (and similar games). Highly skilled and aggressive students tend to dominate this game, while the lesser-skilled players get fewer turns and are at a higher risk of being hit with a ball. Even with the use of nerf balls, it is difficult to make this a developmentally appropriate activity.

- Games such as Steal the Bacon and Line Soccer, in which students are split into teams and assigned numbers. In these games, only two or four students are active at a time, and because the numbers are called at random, the students called may be mismatched in their skill ability or size. In such instances, the disadvantaged students are subject to peer pressure and injury.

If a student feels emotionally threatened by an activity, he or she is unlikely to participate enthusiastically or benefit from the activity. Taking steps to maximize participation and allow each player to feel successful will ensure that all students in your physical education program will thrive.

MODIFYING GAMES TO ACCOMMODATE PLAYERS' NEEDS

If you find that a particular game no longer holds students' interest, is not meeting your intended learning objective, or is not allowing for maximum participation, modifying the game may prove to be a viable solution. The elements of a game that can be altered are usually the desired outcomes, skills involved, equipment used, rules, and the number of players on a team.

Some methods of modifying games are:

- If the game calls for elimination of players, modify the rules to allow them to return to the action quickly.

- Change an individual activity to a partner, small-group, and, finally, a team activity.

- Increase the number of "its." A general rule is one "it" for every five students playing. You can also increase the number of runners.

- Change distances that children have to run or throw.

- Change the locomotor skills children must use. (For example, instead of running, children can skip or hop.)

- Devise new methods of tagging.

- Increase or decrease the size of goals or scoring areas.

- Change the boundaries. Adjust the boundaries to minimize the possibility of players bumping into one another and to reasonably limit the amount of space in which escaping players can move to avoid being tagged.

- Modify the scoring process.

- Alter the amount or type of equipment used.

- Increase or decrease the duration of the game.

- Allow students to suggest methods of modification.

FINDING THE RIGHT GAME

There are many games you can choose to help you achieve your teaching objectives. To help you get started in finding the games you need for a particular event, group, or teaching objective, I've grouped the games in this book into the following categories. Most of the games are low organized games.

Low Organized Games

Everyone who has attempted to categorize low organized games has his or her own system, and every system has its own strong points. The low organized games in this book are categorized as follows:

Movement Awareness Activities: These activities are suitable for any age level and will help students improve their spatial awareness. Activities in this category are a good foundation in the skills needed to ensure safety and generally deal with learning to move and to change direction quickly while avoiding contact with others.

Circle Games: Circle games can be played moving around or across a circle. Players do not have to make many decisions as to where they will move during the game, which keeps the strategy relatively simple. Many circle games, such as *Duck Duck Goose* and *Good Morning,* allow for only two students to be active at a time. Although games of this nature may be appropriate for recreational settings, they do not fit into a success oriented physical education program.

Single Line Games: In single line games, the action takes place with the participants all moving toward the same goal at the same time. These games require a slightly higher level of strategy than circle games because players have to choose a safe path across the playing area to keep from being caught or colliding with other players. Learning to move without colliding with other players is one of the main objectives of single line games.

Double Line Games: In these games, players move in two directions at the same time. This increases the strategy level required because players have to make more decisions in order to move across the playing area safely and successfully.

Tag Games: In tag games, players are in almost constant motion and need to use a lot of strategic thinking in order to move safely and avoid being tagged.

Scatter Games: Scatter games get their classification because they do not have consistent starting formations nor do the players move in common patterns as they do in line games. In addition, players have a lot of freedom regarding where and how they move.

Small Group Games: Small group games include groups of two to five players. These activities are great for encouraging natural leadership and maximizing participation.

Cooperative Games: Cooperative games and tasks emphasize teamwork for the common benefit of the group. These activities necessitate equality, participation, trust, and mutual success.

Games for Improving Eye-Hand Coordination: These games entail contact with a moving object by the hand or with an implement such as a racquet or paddle. These activities promote hand-eye coordination.

High Organized Games

High organized games normally refer to major team sports or games that involve complex or extensive rules. Only mature players can apply the necessary strategy to play these games successfully. Most of the high organized games you will find in this book fall into the lead-up game category.

Lead-Up Games: Games in this category are modifications of major team sports. They are designed to allow players to practice skills pertinent to the sport being taught or to make the game more appropriate for a certain skill or maturity level.

One last section in the book features a variety of activities suitable for play day (also known as field day). Games in this section tend to fit into the recreational games category.

Section 1

MOVEMENT AWARENESS GAMES

In a well-planned and carefully developed physical education program, special movement exploration lessons are used to increase a child's spatial awareness (the ability to move in different directions without bumping into other people or objects). It is important to take the time to enhance children's spatial awareness before introducing them to advanced games, particularly tag and team games. The games in this section are intended to help you meet this objective.

1.   NO TOUCH

Introduction: No-Touch is a game designed for reinforcing moving in general space without colliding with others.

Equipment: None

Game preparation: Designate the area in which the game is to be played, and have players scatter about within the defined area.

Game play: On the start signal, all players move (walk) within the area trying to keep from "touching" any other students. If a player bumps or touches another person, both stop, stand back to back, stare at the floor, count to ten, and then return to participating in the game again.

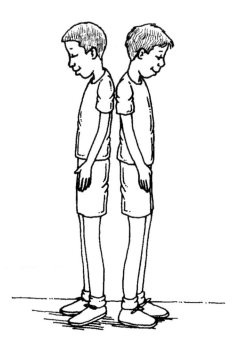

Tips:

- Start with a large play area and progressively decrease it in size.
- As the students develop skill in moving without bumping into one another, change the modes of locomotion. Have the children try hopping, skipping, galloping, or sliding.

2. STATUES

Introduction: This activity reinforces the players' spatial awareness and provides a few laughs. It is also an excellent activity to use as a quick hitter at the beginning of a lesson to energize the students.

Equipment: None

Game preparation: None

Game play: Students begin by walking around in the play area. When you call out a type of statue, everyone is to freeze in a pose that matches the style you have called.

Tip:

- It is easy to use a theme and have all of the statues relate to that theme. Be creative and experiment with a variety of themes. The following may help you get started:

  Sport movements

  Machines

  Cartoon figures

  Alien creatures

  Playing musical instruments

  Performers in the circus

  Feelings

  People at work

3. HIGH FIVES

Introduction: This activity reinforces players' spatial awareness. It is an excellent way to get students energized at the start of class.

Equipment: None

Game preparation: None

Game play: Designate the locomotor skill—walking, skipping, hopping, etc.—you want students to use. Students begin the activity by moving about the play area. When you give the signal, players are to give high-fives to as many students as possible until the signal is given to resume movement in general space. Remind players to time their jumps so they touch hands at the peak of their jump.

Tips:

- Another challenge is for the students to only give high fives right hand to right hand. Later, try left hand to left hand.

- Finish this challenge by telling students to jump off the left foot when they give a high five with the right hand and then jump off the right foot to give the high fives with the left hand. This last challenge makes this drill a lead-up skill for shooting a basketball lay-up shot.

4. SHADOWING

Introduction: This activity is also related to developing movement awareness, but is combined with a challenge, making it thoroughly enjoyable for students— as long as it's played only for a short time period. This is also a good activity to use to lead into playing defense in basketball.

Equipment: None

Game preparation: Pair up all the students, with one player being the leader and the other the shadow for each pair.

Game play: The leaders begin by moving anywhere in the play area as long as they are using a slide. (That forces them to go side to side.). The shadows need to stay as close to their leaders as possible, without touching them. When you give the stop signal, the shadows must be able to take just one step to reach their partners. Reverse roles and play again.

Tips:

- Try the game having the players move at different levels—for example, the leader moving in a fully upright position while the shadows move in low, slightly squatting position, as if they were playing defense in basketball.

- Try playing the game with both players moving only in sliding motions, moving from side to side. This also correlates with playing defense in basketball.

6

5. LIVING LETTERS

Introduction: This is another activity that enhances spatial awareness skills, but because it involves group cooperation and a bit of competition, students find it particularly appealing.

Equipment: None

Game preparation: None

Game play: Students are to move around the play area using a designated locomotor skill, such as hopping or skipping. When you call out a number and a letter, students are to get into groups of the number you called, then use all the members of the group to form the letter you called. For example, if you call 3A, students are to first get into groups of three, then use all three people to make the letter A. If you call 4N, the students are to get into groups of four, and then make the letter N, using all of the people in the group.

Tips:

- You can award points to the first group to finish each challenge, or just wait for all of the groups to complete the task and move on to the next challenge.

- Advanced students could try and make a word with the number of people specified.

6. DAYTONA SPEEDWAY

Grades 1–6

Introduction: This is a movement awareness activity that students particularly enjoy. Just a few well-chosen words about the fact that the Daytona Speedway is the world's fastest race are usually enough to trigger the imagination of elementary age youngsters.

Equipment: None

Game preparation: Arrange the players around the perimeter of a square area (at least 30' × 30') and space them evenly. Tell players that they are driving a car on the Daytona Speedway, and that the important thing in finishing this race is to never have an accident.

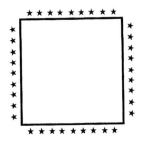

Game play: In preparation for the big race, the drivers must master the first three tasks before tackling the fourth task, the big race.

1. Students along one pair of opposite lines of the square are challenged to exchange places without bumping into anyone. Have the other two lines repeat the task. Try this at various speeds and with different locomotor skills.

2. Students along both pairs of opposing lines (all four lines) are to exchange places without bumping into anyone.

3. All drivers enter the driving area and move continuously in any direction, while never touching anyone. As they explore the area, establish three gears: first gear (very slow); second gear (move at a jog); third gear (move at a run). Try the same activity using different locomotor skills and adjust the gears accordingly.

   Once students have mastered these three skills, they are ready for the fourth skill, the race itself.

4. Moving throughout the play space, drivers must try and touch all four lines and get back to their starting spot without colliding with anyone.

Tips:

- If the class is really good, you can have students try to make two laps (touch each side two times) without touching any other participant.

- Students involved in a collision put their hands up by their ears and go "beep — beep—beep" all the way back to their original starting spot. The "beeps" show that a particular vehicle is under tow and that other drivers must use caution around this vehicle.

7. MOTORCYCLE RACE

Introduction: Motorcycle Race is an extension of Daytona Speedway but involves an element of cooperation, because it is performed in pairs.

Equipment: None

Game preparation: The starting formation is the same as Daytona Speedway (see page 8) except that now everyone lines up with a partner. The partner standing in front extends his or her arms backward to create motorcycle handlebars, and the person in the back, the driver, holds on to the handlebars.

Game play: When you give the start signal, drivers must steer their motorcycles across to the other line and back home, without bumping into other motorcycles. When players master that task, they can try to steer their motorcycle around all four sides of the course without touching another motorcycle.

Tips:

- If a collision occur, place participants under tow as in Daytona Speedway.

- If certain sets of partners repeatedly "crash," they should sit out and watch the safe drivers on the course for a specific time.

- When the class becomes skilled at this game, have the students playing the part of the motorcycle close their eyes. This is referred to as driving with the "lights off." Emphasize that success in this mode requires cooperation, not speed. Caution students to be extra careful when in this "lights off" challenge.

8. STOCK CAR RACE

Grades 2–6

Introduction: Stock Car Race is a variation of the Motorcycle Race (see page 9). Along with enhancing spatial awareness skills, it offers players an opportunity to work with a partner and learn the value of cooperation.

Equipment: None

Game preparation: Group children in pairs and have the partners stand one in front of the other outside of the square area as described in Daytona Speedway (see page 8). The person in front is the stock car; the one in the rear is the driver. The stock cars raise both arms with elbows bent to shoulder height, thus, "bumpers" are ready. The drivers place both of their hands on the stock cars' shoulders to guide the stock cars.

Game play: First ask for the stock car to be driven across to the opposite line and back without touching any other stock car. Once players master that task have all 4 lines go to the opposite line and back safely at the same time. Try having students touch all four sides as they drive in any direction inside the course.

Tips

- If a collision occurs, all players involved must use a tow truck to return to their starting place and start over.

- The first stock car across and back home successfully without touching anyone is declared the winner for that race.

- Try playing this game with the stock cars' lights off (eyes closed).

9. BUMPER CARS

Introduction: Bumper Cars is another variation of Motorcycle Race and offers an opportunity to cooperatively work with a partner. It should not be interpreted as bumper cars on the carnival midway where the cars bump into each other on purpose.

Equipment: None

Game preparation: Start out with the same formation as in Daytona Speedway (see page 8), except that now everyone lines up with a partner. Partners face each other and place their hands on each other's shoulders. Bumpers become each person's bottom. One person assumes the role of driver and the other person has the role of the car.

Game play: First ask for the car to be driven across to the opposite line and back without bumping any other car. Once players master that task, have all four lines cross at the same time. Lastly have the students touch all four lines as they drive in any direction inside the course and return to their home.

Tips:

- If a collision occurs, all involved must use a tow truck to return to their starting place and start over.

- The first bumper car to complete the designated race successfully without touching anyone and go back home is declared the winner for that race.

- Try playing this game with the lights off (eyes closed).

10. BIG MACK TRUCK RACE

Grades 3–6

Introduction: Like many of the other games presented in this section, along with enhancing spatial skills, this game also encourages cooperation. The game is based upon the same principles as the Stock Car Race (see page 10), except this time four players work together.

Equipment: None

Game preparation: Start out with the same formation as for Stock Car Race, but make Big Mack Trucks by putting students into groups of four, with two students in the back and two in the front of each group. Both pairs of students link inside elbows, then the students in the back—that is, in the Big Mack cab—place their hands on the front couples' shoulders. The students in front raise their free arms for bumpers.

Game play: On the start signal, players must race across the floor to the opposite line and return home again. Once players have mastered that, challenge them further by having the trucks race one lap, touching all four lines of the square and returning home.

Tips:

- The truck to complete the designated task first without colliding with other trucks is the winner.

- For extra excitement allow the students to sound off like big diesel horns when another truck gets in their way.

- Try playing this game while having the front couples keep their lights off (eyes closed) and rely upon the drivers for guidance.

Section 2

CIRCLE GAMES

Circle games get their name because the starting formation is always a circle. For young children being introduced to group games, circle games are very helpful because they provide a definite area to play in or around. This gives them a sense of security in where to move.

It is very difficult to find developmentally appropriate circle games for any age or skill level, which is why so few games appear in this section.

Circle games that *are* presented range from the very simple games to those that can challenge older students.

11. OBJECTELEPHANTITUS

Grades K–2

Introduction: This game will help students develop finger coordination and eye-hand coordination. It also stimulates the imagination.

Equipment:

- a variety of different shaped and sized objects (such as erasers, pennies, rhythm sticks, balls, etc.)

Game preparation: Have children sit in a circle, then distribute the objects among the players in the circle.

Game play: When you give the start signal, the children are to quickly pass the objects around the circle, with each child handing the object to the child next to him or her, without dropping it. If an object is dropped, the child who dropped it must pick it up and pass it on to the next person. When the signal to stop is given, those with an object in their hands are Objectelephantitus (a nonsense word to identify the children caught with objects in their hands.) No stigma is attached to being termed Objectelephantitus because eventually all the players will be caught.

Tips:

- The signal to start and stop should be musical.

- Have players caught with objects in their hands go to the middle of the circle and perform a task, such as acting like a monkey for ten seconds or doing five jumping jacks. As soon as a child performs the assigned task, he or she is free of objectelephantitus and can rejoin the circle. Then you can start the game all over again

12. COLOR MIX

Introduction: Color Mix will help children develop coordination and is an excellent game for youngsters learning the names of colors.

Equipment:

- colored spot for each player (a large variety of poly spots works best, but construction paper taped to the floor will also work; use four to six different colors)

Game preparation: Arrange colored spots (one for each child except the one who's "it" around a circle about 22' in diameter (as shown in the diagram). Use one color for every five children playing.

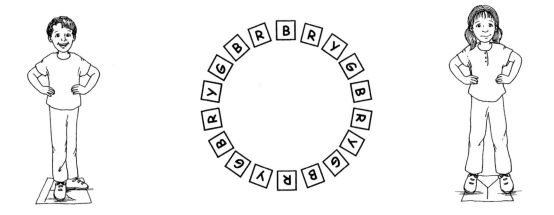

Game play: All participants but one "it" stand on a colored spot. As you call out two or more colors, the children on those colors must all trade places and find a new color. As the exchange is being made, "it" attempts to take a color place. The player not getting a color spot is "it."

Tip:

- Once the children have gotten the hang of the game, make it more challenging by calling out "Spill the paint" to have everyone in the circle look for a new spot.

13. MOUSETRAP

Introduction: Along with being entertaining, this game helps children develop agility.

Equipment: None

Game preparation: Divide players into two groups. Have one group make a hand-held circle representing the mousetrap, while the other group—the mice—scatters around the outside of the circle.

Game play: One person, either you or a player, must be "it." This person stands with his or her back to the mousetrap . When "it" says "Open," the children in the circle raise their arms, "opening the mouse trap." The mice then run in and out of the circle as often as they dare. When "it" says "close," the children lower their arms, closing the mousetrap. Any mice caught inside then join the mousetrap circle.

Tips:

- Designate a time limit or number of turns for each group. When the time is up, congratulate those who were not caught. Switch groups and begin again.

14. SPACESHIP

Introduction: Spaceship allows students to practice running, as well as starting and stopping on a signal.

Equipment: None

Game preparation: Arrange players evenly around a circle about 25′ in diameter. Assign each player a spaceship name such as Nautilus, Jupiter, Mercury, Saturn, and Explorer. Use the same name for every four or five players.

Game play: Stand in the middle of the circle and tell students you represent the Earth. As you call out the name of one of the spaceships those students "blast-off" and begin running around the circle (orbiting the Earth). They're to keep running until you call "touchdown." At that time, the students must cut through the circle and run and tag your outstretched hand, then go back to their starting spots. You can then call a new spaceship name.

Tips:

- Caution runners to slow down before reaching you.

- If you keep students moving at a fast pace, they won't have to wait long for new turns. Young students love to run, so their enthusiasm will be high.

- If the students really understand the game, call more than one spaceship at a time.

15. HORSE AND JOCKEY

Grades 2–6

Introduction: This game can lead into an excellent discussion of learning to bear weight on your own body.

Equipment: None

Game preparation: Have students form a double circle, with those on the inside facing their partners in the outside circle. The people on the outside stand with their legs straddled wide apart.

Game play: On the signal "go," the inside people crawl through their partners' legs (the starting gates) and race clockwise around the circle. Once the inside student has left the gate, his or her partner gets down on all fours like a horse. Upon returning to their partners, the runners mount them, like jockeys mounting their horses. The first couple mounted as horse and jockey are the winners.

Tips:

- Discussing the starting gates at a horse-racing track is an interesting way to introduce this game.
- With a little imagination, you can find endless variations for this game. Here are a few to get you started:
  - Have the jockey leap-frog over the horse and finish sitting cross-legged fashion on the ground facing the middle of the circle.
  - Have the jockey mount the horse piggy-back style.
  - Have the horse pick up the jockey in a fireman's carry.
- Safety Note: All stunts used to end each race should be taught and practiced prior to being used as part of this game.

16.   CIRCLE CHASE

Introduction: Circle Chase challenges students to respond to auditory signals quickly and to be able to accelerate rapidly in speed.

Equipment: None

Game preparation: Have participants stand in a circle and number off by fives.

Game play: As you call out a number from one to five, all players with that number race counter-clockwise around the circle trying to get back to their spot without being tagged by another runner. A player who gets tagged drops out for that lap and exits by moving to the inside of the circle to return to his or her starting spot. Players are to keep track of the number of times they were tagged. At the conclusion of the playing time, those who were tagged the least are the winners.

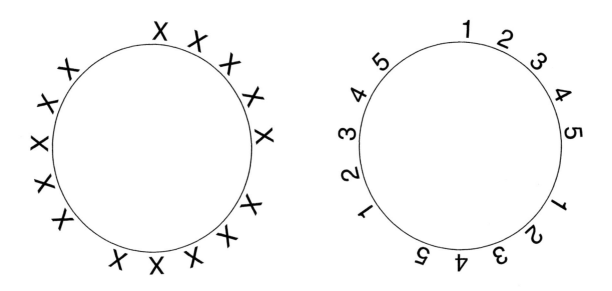

Tips:

- After every few rounds have students change places and renumber.
- For a faster-paced game, have players run two laps instead of one and call more than one number at a time.

17. SHOE PASS

Introduction: This fast-moving game is good for developing abdominal fitness. It is not your typical circle game but it is a great class cooperative experience that fosters camaraderie.

Equipment:

- each student's right shoe

Game preparation: Have players sit in a circle, with their knees raised as in a curl-up. Space the players so they are almost touching shoulders. Players are to take off their right shoe and hold it in their right hand.

Game play: As you call out count 1 through 4, everyone must perform the following routine:

Count 1: Touch shoe to floor by right foot

Count 2: Lay down and touch shoe to floor over head

Count 3: Curl-up; touch the shoe to floor in front by the right foot again

Count 4: Pass the shoe under your legs to the person on your left; pick up the shoe passed to you

Repeat the above sequence until shoes have traveled around the circle back to their owners

Tips:

- The goal of the activity is to see if all the players in the group get their own shoes back. If they all get them back at the same time, it is considered above average. Regardless of the outcome, all of the players will have exercised their abdominal muscles.

Section 3

SINGLE LINE GAMES

Single line games are so named because all participants are moving toward the same goal at the same time. You will notice that some games in this section, such as Black Bear, are played using two lines, but attention is only given to one line at a time.

Single line games allow for a somewhat wider range of movements than do most circle games, but are still simple and contained.

In the single line games you'll find in this section, all players are involved at all times. For this reason, children particularly enjoy these games. They especially like it when the teacher or leader joins in and assumes the role of "it," as in the role of "Bulldog" in the game Midnight.

The author has tried to list the games in order, from easy to more difficult.

18. OCTOPUS

Introduction: Explain to students that an octopus has several tentacles or arms that allow it to reach out to grab things.

Equipment: None

Game preparation: Have all the players line up on a line at the outside of the playing area. Set up another line at least 35' to 40' long at the opposite end of the playing area for the children to run to.

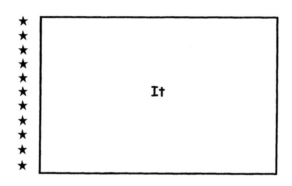

Game play: Choose one player to be the octopus ("it"). The octopus takes a position in the middle of the playing area.

When you say "Everyone must swim through the ocean," all of the players must run across to the other line. The octopus tries to tag as many people as possible. Players who get tagged become tentacles of the octopus. They may not move from the spot where they were tagged, but when a player comes close to them, they can reach out and tag that player, who then also becomes a tentacle.

Tips:

- The octopus may always move freely. As more players become tentacles, a smart octopus will manipulate his or her quarry into a group of strategically positioned tentacles.

19. MIDNIGHT

Introduction: This game helps students develop speed and agility through a dramatization of the age-old feud between cats and dogs.

Equipment: None

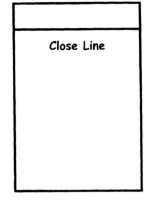

Game preparation: Mark a line at one endo of the playing area to be the cats' fence posts, and another line 30' to 40' away for the bulldog's house. A line 3' to 4' away from the bulldog's house is called the close line.

Select one player to be "it," or Mr. Bulldog, and have that player stand in the bulldog house. All the other players are cats, and stand on the line representing their fence posts or safe spots.

Designate one cat as the leader.

Game play: The leader cat signals and leads all of the cats to the close line for the purpose of teasing the bulldog. The leader cat asks Mr. (Mrs.) Bulldog, "What time is it, Mr. Bulldog?" and Mr. Bulldog answers, "One o'clock" or any time. The leader cat continues to repeat the question until Mr. Bulldog answers "Midnight." On that signal Mr. Bulldog chases all of the cats back to their fence posts. All of the cats tagged by the bulldog go to the bulldog house and become Mr. Bulldog's helpers. If the leader cat is caught, he or she chooses a new cat to become the leader.

Tips:

- This game continues until a desired number of cats are left. Depending on the number of players, it may be a good idea to stop when ten cats are left and start a new game. This also helps with safety.

- A safety precaution is to have the cats start from a sideways starting position when they are at the close line. This will eliminate some collisions as runners return to their safe line.

20. THE THREE BEARS

Introduction: This take-off on the story of *Goldilocks and the Three Bears* helps students develop speed and agility.

Equipment: None

Game preparation: Play the game on a floor marked out as for the game *Midnight* (see page 26).

Choose three children to represent each of the three bears: Mama Bear, Papa Bear, and Baby Bear. Have the bears stand close together at the line behind the close line, facing the other players, who are the Goldilocks. You stand behind the bears.

Game play: On the start signal, the Goldilocks leave their line and go to the close line by the bears. They ask "Who's at Home?" You secretly touch one of the bears, and that bear answers Goldilocks' question. If Baby Bear answers, "Baby Bear," they ask again. If Mama Bear answers, "Mama Bear," they ask again. If Papa Bear answers, "Papa Bear!" all players turn and run back to their safe line. All three bears chase them. Any players who get tagged return to the bears' line and help the Three Bears catch the remaining players. Only the original Three Bears answer the question "Who's there?"

Tips:

- The game continues until a desired number of Goldilocks are left. Depending on the number of players, you can choose to stop when about ten Goldilocks are left and start a new game, selecting new bears.

- Because the game is based on the story of *Goldilocks and the Three Bears,* a review of the story is an excellent method of introducing the game.

21. LITTLE BROWN BEAR

Introduction: Little Brown Bear is a great method of practicing and reviewing locomotor skills.

Equipment: None

Game preparation: Mark off two parallel lines 30′ to 40′ long, and at least 40′ apart. The area between the two end lines represents the "woods." The children must all line up on one line. Choose one or two players to be Little Brown Bear, or "it."

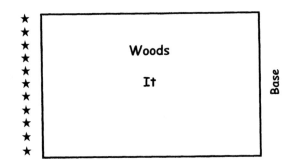

Game play: Little Brown Bear calls, "Who's afraid of the Little Brown Bear?" The children answer, "Not me." Little Brown Bear then replies, "Then you must *skip* through the woods." All of the children must skip through the woods as Little Brown Bear stated. Using the same locomotor skill, Little Brown Bear must try to tag as many players as possible as they move through the woods. Players who are tagged become Little Brown Bear's helpers.

Tips:

- When there are about ten players left select a new Little Brown Bear and repeat the game.

- Little Brown Bear may call any locomotor skill, including walk, run, gallop, hop, jump, or slide. You can also be creative and add choices such as "drive" or "go by plane." Brown Bear and his helpers must use the same locomoter skill as the other players.

22. MARTIANS

Introduction: Along with being a good game for helping students develop speed and agility, this is also a good way for younger students to review colors.

Equipment: None

Game preparation: Designate a playing area at least 35′ × 45′ and mark off a line on one end of the area. Choose one player to be a Martian ("it") and stand in the middle of the playing area. The remainder of the class, the Earthlings, must stand on one end line.

Game play: The Earthlings chant, "Martian, Martian, will you take us to the Stars?" The Martian replies, "Yes, if you are wearing red (or any color the Martian chooses to call out)." Players wearing the designated color may then walk safely across the playing area. The remainder of the class can run across to try and reach the other side safely. Any players who are caught must join the Martian and help catch the other players.

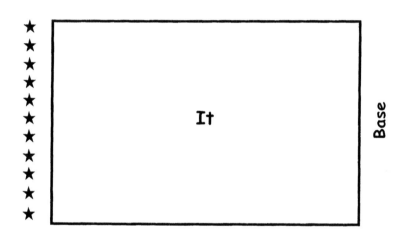

Tips:

- It's helpful to review that Martians come from the planet Mars so that the word makes sense to the students.

- Depending on the size of the group, when there are about ten players left, select a new Martian and repeat the game.

29

23. BLACK BEAR

Grades 1–3

Introduction: Black Bear is a game that tests auditory discrimination and teaches children to navigate a designated area while avoiding being tagged. Anticipating the signal adds to the fun.

Equipment: None

Game preparation: Designate a playing area and mark off two parallel lines 30′ to 40′ long, or the length of the gym, and at least 40′ feet apart. Choose one child to be Black Bear, or "it," and have him or her stand in the center of the area. Have all the other players stand along the base line.

Game play: Any time Black Bear calls "Black Bear, Black Bear, Black Bear," all of the players must try to run across to the opposite line without being tagged. Those who are tagged become Black Bear's helpers and must help tag the other players.

Black Bear may try to trick the runners by calling different colors such as "Black Bear, Black Bear, Green Bear." If a player makes a false start on anything but the words "Black Bear, Black Bear, Black Bear," that person must become one of Black Bear's helpers.

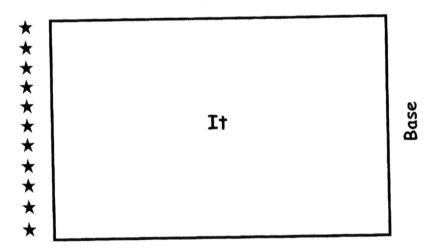

Tips:
- Play until about half of the players have been caught and then start over.

24. SPIDERS AND FLIES

Introduction: This game offers more freedom of movement for the participants because they now have a choice of which goal to run to for safety.

Equipment: None

Game preparation: Designate a playing area about 40' x 40' in size, and mark off lines on all four sides. These will serve as flies' bases. Mark off a circle 5' to 10' in diameter in the center of the playing area. This will be the spider's web. Select one player to be the first spider and go to the center of the spider's web. (Sometimes it is good to have more than one spider to start the game.) The spider must squat down and keep his or her eyes closed. All of the other players line up along the base lines and assume the role of flies.

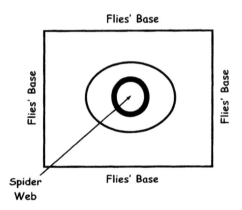

Game play: On the start signal, the flies sneak out to the spider's web. When the spider thinks the flies are close enough to catch, he or she can spring up and chase them. The flies may seek refuge at either base line. The flies that are caught return to the spider's web and become the spider's helpers. The spider's helpers do not have to keep their eyes closed, but none of them may take off to chase flies until the spider begins the chase.

Tips:

- If the flies are unwilling to get close enough to the spider's web use a "close circle." Now every fly must get on the "close circle," before the spiders can chase.

- Play until one fly or a small group of flies remains. Flies who were not caught can be declared the winners.

25. ACROSS THE GREAT DIVIDE

Grades 2–5

Introduction: Here is a challenging single line game for players who are "it."

Equipment: None

Game preparation: Mark two parallel lines about 15′ apart across the middle of the playing area to represent the Great Divide. Mark off the outer boundaries of the playing area parallel to the Great Divide to designate the run-to lines. Select one person to be "it" and stand in the middle of the Great Divide, and have all of the remaining players line up at one end of the playing area. The "it" must always stay between the two lines (the Great Divide).

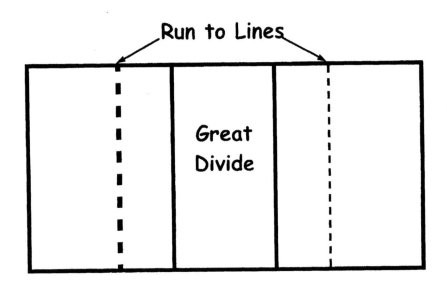

Game play: When "it" calls "Westward Ho," all of the players must cross the Great Divide to reach the other side. Any player tagged by the "it" in the Great Divide becomes an "it." The "its" must join hands and stay together in the Great Divide at all times. Only the original "it" can call "Westward Ho."

Tips:

- Have players run to the outer lines even though they are safe as soon as they are out of the Great Divide.
- Play until most of the players have been tagged.

26. WHITE BEAR

Grades 1–3

Introduction: This game provides an opportunity to move in general space with a partner, without colliding with others.

Equipment: None

Game preparation: Designate a playing area and mark off base lines on parallel sides of that area. Have all of the children, who represent the fish, line up on one end of that area. The inside of the playing area is the Arctic Ocean. Mark off a small area in the middle of the sea to be an ice cave where White Bear lives. Select one person to be White Bear and stand on the piece of ice.

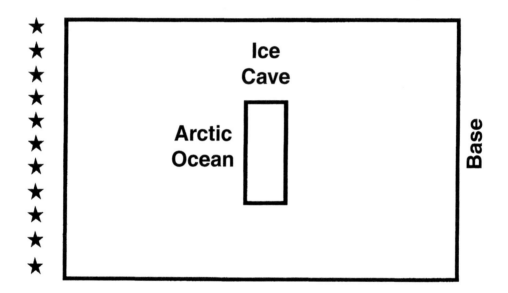

Game play: Whenever White Bear says "White Bear is hungry," all of the fish must run across the sea area and attempt to reach the opposite base line as White Bear chases them. White Bear may only catch one fish each time. The fish caught by White Bear go to the bear's ice cave. White Bear then gives the signal and goes fishing again. Whenever White Bear has a pair of fish in the ice cave, they join hands and become a fishermen. It takes two fisherman holding hands to make one fisherman. Then when White Bear calls out "White Bear is hungry," the fishermen do the fishing and White Bear stays home. Each pair of captured fish must always keep their hands joined. Like the bear, they are only allowed to catch one fish at a time and they must take fish they catch to the ice cave.

Tips:

- This continues until all but a few fish have been caught.

27. SHARKS AND SEALS

Introduction: This is a basic single line game that introduces an element of strategy.

Equipment:

- five poly spots

Game preparation: Designate a playing area and mark off base lines on opposing sides of the area. Scatter the poly spots in the playing area to represent islands of safety. Select two or three players to be sharks, and have them stand in the middle of the playing area. The remaining players, the seals, line up on one of the base lines.

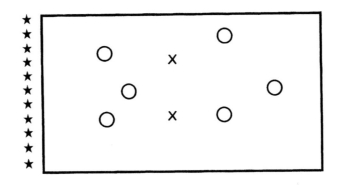

Game play: The sharks call to the seals and beckon them to cross to the other line. Any seal that is caught becomes a shark. A seal who has one foot on an island is safe and may stay on the island until all of the seals are told to run to the other line again. More than one person may occupy an island, as long as they can get one foot on it.

Tips:

- Play until only a few seals remain, then select new sharks and start the game again.

28. BIG FOOT

Introduction: This game gets its name because the "its" will be using their big foot to catch the players as they cross the playing area.

Equipment:

- one soccer ball (or rubber ball of approximately the same size) per player.

Game preparation: Designate a playing area and mark off base lines on opposing sides of that area. Choose one player to be Big Foot, or "it," and take a spot in the middle of the playing area in crab walk position. All other players stand with a ball on a line at one end of the playing area.

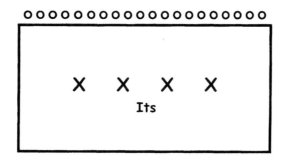

Game play: Big Foot does not have a ball. When Big Foot gives the signal "Big Foot is coming!" players must dribble their balls soccer-style across the playing area to the other boundary. They wait there for the next signal to return. Big Foot catches the dribblers by knocking their ball away, using only his or her feet to do this. A player whose ball gets taken away becomes a Big Foot and helps catch the remaining players.

Tips:

- Play until five to ten players remain and then reorganize and start a new game.
- Try starting the game with more than one Big Foot.
- Have players use different ball skills (such as dribbling basketball style) to get across the playing area.
- Floor hockey dribbling may also be tried, with the "its" using sticks to intercept the dribblers instead of using the crab walk.

29.   FISH NET

Grades 3–5

Introduction: Teamwork and an element of team strategy are necessary for success in this game, making it the most difficult single line game in this chapter.

Equipment: None

Game preparation: Designate a playing area and mark off base lines on opposing sides of that area. (Unless the gym is extremely large, this game is best played using the perimeter of the gym as the boundaries.) Divide the players into two teams and select a player from each team to be the captain. Have each team stand along a base line at one end of the playing area. Designate one team as the fish net and have all members of that team join hands to make one long line. The players on the other line are the fish and they move individually.

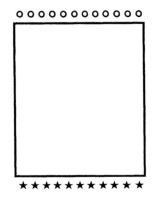

Game play: When you say "Go," both teams run toward the center. The net tries to catch as many fish as possible by making a circle around them. The fish try to avoid getting caught by getting out of the opening of the net before it closes. They may not go under the arms of the net or break through the net. They may go through the net if the net breaks because the players let go of hands. The fish are safe if they get to the opposite goal line without being caught. When the net has made its circle, the captain of the fish net team counts the number of fish inside the net and tells the teacher the score. The teams now change roles and repeat the procedure. The fish caught return to their team after the count is taken.

When each side has had a chance to be the net three times, the game is over and the team with the highest score for all three turns wins.

36

30. FROGGY

Introduction: Along with teaching agility and strategy, this game teaches students about how wildlife must confront their ever-changing habitats.

Equipment:
- three or four hoops
- cones
- three tumbling mats
- five or six carpet squares

Game preparation: Designate a playing area and mark off a starting line on one end of that area. Use the hoops to represent lily pads, cones to represent trees, tumbling mats to represent ditches, and carpet squares to represent rocks. Place these in the playing area as shown in the diagram below.

Select eight players to be the "its," and assign them to be pairs of the following: cars, trucks, snakes, and alligators. Have each pair stand together in a zone along the ditches, trees, etc. (See the diagram.) The "its" must stay in their zones at all times. The remaining players are the frogs and they line up at the starting line.

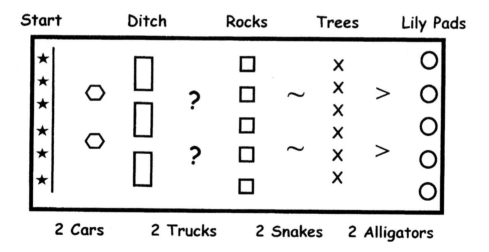

Game play: Frogs must escape many dangers, including those caused by people, such as traffic, as well as their natural enemies. The ditches, rocks, and trees are safe areas, but the froggies' ultimate goal is to reach the lily pads. Beginning at the starting line, the froggies may try to advance to a new level of safety whenever they feel they can make it without being caught. If a frog is in a safety zone they may stay there indefinitely. Froggies that are tagged by an "it" must return to the starting line and begin again. To keep the game moving, after a frog reaches a lily pad, he or she could take the place of an "it" and the "it" could start as a frog.

31. HOT WEATHER TAG

Grades 3–6

Introduction: This fun hot weather game will enhance children's running ability.

Equipment:

- one or two buckets filled with water
- one very small paper cup for each player

Game preparation: Designate a playing area and mark off base lines along opposing sides of the area. Place the buckets in the middle of the playing area. Choose one or two students to be "it." Give them each a cup of water and have them stand in the middle of the playing area. Have the remainder of the players line up on one of the base lines.

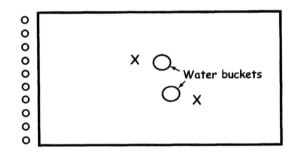

Game play: When you say "It's time to cool off," all of the players must try to reach the other end of the playing area without being splashed. Any player splashed by an "it" becomes a new "it" and receives a cup of water. The "its" may only fill their water cup once each time the players run across the playing area.

Tips:

- Stop the game when only five or so players are still dry, and start over again with new "its."
- It's best if you first have all players agree that no one will try to get wet on purpose.

Section 4

DOUBLE LINE GAMES

Double Line Games get their classification because action is taking place from two opposing lines at the same time. The game of "Touchdown" is an excellent example of a Double Line Game. In this game, one team is moving forward and trying to cross the opposing team's goal line, while the second team is trying to prevent people from crossing their goal line.

Double line games are more complex in nature than single line games and quite often involve some degree of strategy. As you will notice, most double line games are recommended for second grade and higher. When using these games with second graders, it's best to wait until the later part of the school year, when children have developed more maturity and more advanced movement skills.

The games in this section are organized in a reasonable order of progression from easy to more difficult.

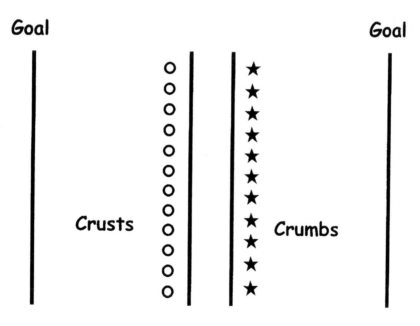

32. MARCH ATTACK

Introduction: This is the first in a series of similar games that allow children to practice quick starts in either of two directions.

Equipment: None

Game preparation: Designate a playing area, and mark off lines on opposing ends of the area.

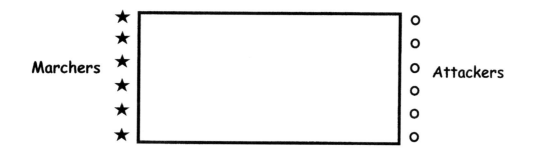

Marchers ★ ★ ★ ★ ★ ★   o o o o o o   Attackers

Game play: Divide players into two teams, the Marchers and the Attackers and have the teams line up on opposing ends of the playing area.

On the command "March," the Marchers begin marching toward the other team (the Attackers). The marching team cannot stop their advance and must continue marching until the signal "attack" is given. At that time, the Attackers chase the Marchers in an attempt to tag players before they reach their home base. Players who are tagged join the opposing team. The two teams return to their respective lines and prepare for the next march. At this time, teams switch roles and the game continues until one team has captured all of the other team's players.

Tip:

- As an alternative, consider setting a time limit before starting the game, with the team with the most players declared the winner at the end of that time.

33. CROWS AND CRANES

Grades 2–6

Introduction: Crows and Cranes has been around for many years. It allows children to practice quick starts in either of two directions and to learn to discriminate between like sounds.

Equipment: None

Game preparation: Designate a playing area and mark off two goal lines at either end of the area. Make two additional lines 3' to 4' apart in the center of the playing area, parallel to the goal lines. Divide players into two teams—the Cranes and the Crows—and have them line up facing each other on the center lines. A caller, either you or a student, stands at the edge of the playing area between the center lines, facing the two groups.

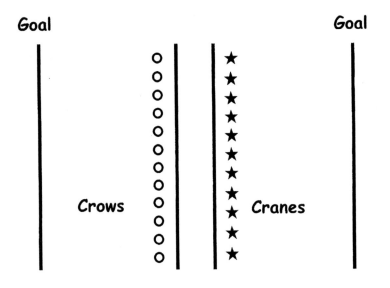

Game play: The caller calls out either "Crows" or "Cranes." If the signal "Crows" is given, the Crows need to run to the boundary line behind them and the Cranes must chase them. If the signal "Cranes" is given, the Cranes need to run to the boundary line behind them and the Crows must chase them.

Any player caught changes teams. A player may end up changing teams several times during the course of a game.

The game continues until all of one team has been captured.

Tips:

- Consider setting a time limit before starting the game. At the end of the designated time the team with the most players is the winner.
- To make the game more exciting the caller can vary the calls by holding onto the Cr-r-r or by adding some distracters such as crackers, cradles, crickets or crab apples before calling out either Cranes or Crows.

34. CRUSTS, CRUMBS, AND CRABS

Grades 2–6

Introduction: This game is an adaptation of the old standby Crows & Cranes, but with new terminology to spice up the game. This game will help students practice quick starts in either direction and discriminate between like sounds.

Equipment: None

Game preparation: Designate a playing area and mark off two goal lines at either end of the area. Make two additional lines 3' to 4' apart in the center of the playing area, parallel to the goal lines. Divide players into two teams—the Crusts and the Crumbs—and have them line up facing each other on the center lines. A caller, either you or a student, stands at the edge of the playing area between the center lines, facing the two groups.

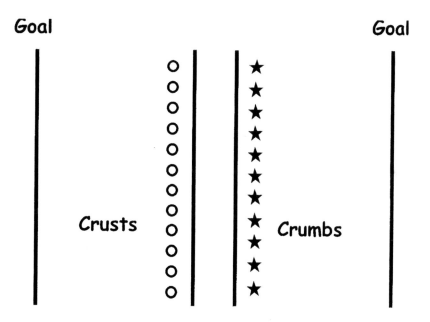

Game play: The caller calls out either "Crusts" or "Crumbs." If the signal "Crusts" is given, the Crusts need to run to the boundary line behind them and the Crumbs must chase them. If the signal "Crumbs" is given, the Crumbs need to run to the boundary line behind them and the Crusts must chase them.

If the signal "Crabs" is given, players on both teams are to kneel on one knee. Those who miss the command and make a false start move to the opposing team.

Tips:

- Consider setting a time limit before starting the game. At the end of the designated time the team with the most players is the winner.

35. CONSONANTS, VOWELS, AND NUMBERS

Introduction: A modification of Crusts, Crumbs and Crabs, this game provides an opportunity to link language arts and physical education together.

Equipment: None

Game preparation: Designate a playing area and mark off two goal lines at either end of the area. Make two additional lines 3' to 4' apart in the center of the playing area, parallel to the goal lines. Divide players into two teams—the Consonants and the Vowels—and have them line up facing each other on the center lines. A caller, either you or a student, stands at the edge of the playing area between the center lines, facing the two groups.

Game play: The caller calls out letters. If a consonant is called, such as "m," the consonants must all run to their bases, and the vowels must try to tag them; if a vowel is called, such as "e," the vowels must run to their base, with the consonants chasing them. A player who is tagged goes to the opposing team's side. If a number is called, players on both teams are to kneel on one knee. The penalty for those who miss the command and make a false start is to move to the opposing team.

Tips:

- Consider setting a time limit before starting the game. At the end of the designated time the team with the most players is the winner.

36. ODDS AND EVENS

Introduction: Odds and Evens is similar to Crusts, Crumbs, and Crabs, except it is played with numbers instead of words. It provides an opportunity to reinforce a basic math concept in physical education.

Equipment:

- 1 or 2 large dice (8-inch square)

Game preparation: Designate a playing area and mark off two goal lines at either end of the area. Make two additional lines 3′ to 4′ apart in the center of the playing area, parallel to the goal lines. Divide players into two teams, the "Odds" and the "Evens."

Game play: Roll the die in the middle between the two teams to determine which team needs to run to their base. If the die comes up odd, the odd team runs and the even team chases. If the die comes up even, the Even team runs and the odd team chases. Any player who is tagged becomes part of the other team.

The game continues until all of one team has been captured.

Tips:

- Consider setting a time limit before starting the game. At the end of the designated time the team with the most players is the winner.

- Try playing the game with two dice, which would require the players to add to determine whether the call is even or odd.

- Try using two dice but having players subtract to figure out whether the call is even or odd.

- Multiplication provides more even answers than odd answers, so it would not be a viable option.

37. STATES, CAPITOLS, AND COUNTRIES

Grades 2–6

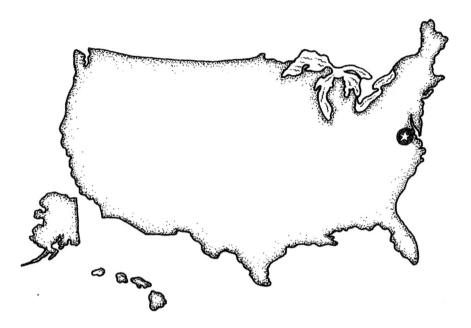

Introduction: This game is based on Crusts, Crumbs and Crabs. It offers the opportunity to link physical education with a social studies lesson.

Equipment: None

Game preparation: Use the same set-up as for Crusts, Crumbs, and Crabs (see page 43). Divide players into two teams—the States and the Capitols—and have them line up facing each other on the center lines. A caller, either you or a student, stands at the edge of the playing area between the center lines, facing the two groups.

Game play: The caller calls out either the name of a state, such as Montana, or the name of a Capitol, such as Olympia. If a state name is called, players in the states group must run to their base line as the Capitols try to tag them. If the name of a Capitol is called, players in the Capitols must try to reach their base line before the states can tag them.

If the name of a country—Germany, for example—is called, players on both teams are to kneel on one knee. Those who miss the command and make a false start move to the opposing team.

The game continues until all of one team has been captured after a designated time.

- Tips: Consider setting a time limit before starting the game.
- Variations on this game can include Carbohydrates, Proteins and Junk Food or Fruits, Vegetables and Junk Food. Be creative in coming up with other themes.

38. SNIPES AND SNORPS

Grades 2–6

Introduction: This is another form of Crusts, Crumbs and Crabs and is played by those rules. The big change is that now the players are starting from a lying down position, making the game much harder.

Equipment: None

Game preparation: Use the same set-up as for Crusts, Crumbs, and Crabs. (see page 43). Divide players into two teams—the Snipes and the Snorps—and have them take their spots along the center lines, and lie down on their backs with their heads about one foot apart. Stand at the edge of the playing area between the center lines, facing the two groups.

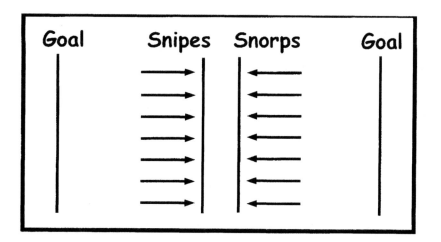

Game play: Randomly call out either Snipes or Snorps. If you call out "Snipes," players in that group must try to reach their base line before the Snorps can tag them; if you call out "Snorps," players in that group must run to safety.

Any player who gets tagged by the opposite team becomes a member of that team. A player may end up changing teams several times during the course of a game.

The game continues until all of one team has been captured.

Tips:

• Consider setting a time limit before starting the game.

39. THE GREAT WALL

Grades 2–5

Introduction: The Great Wall in this game represents the Great Wall of China. This game presents an opportunity to teach students a brief lesson about China.

Equipment: None

Game preparation: Designate a playing area and mark off two base lines at either end of the area. Make two additional lines 15 feet to 20 feet apart in the center of the playing area, parallel to the goal lines. The area inside the inner lines is the Great Wall. Choose one person to be the Wall guard, or "it." All other players line up along either base line.

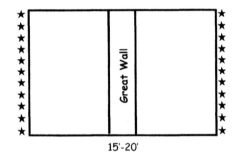

15'-20'

Game play: When you give the start signal, players try to cross the wall and the guard tries to capture (tag) them. The guard may only capture people within the "Great Wall." Any player who is captured becomes another guard on the wall. Players may cross the Great Wall at will. They do not have to wait for a specific signal to cross.

Tips:

- Play continues until about two thirds of the players have been caught. At that point the game should be terminated, as it may be a safety hazard to continue.

- The winners are the players who were not captured.

- Sometimes it is difficult for the first guard to catch anyone, so make sure that the first guard is fairly agile.

40. EMERGENCY

Grades 3–6

Introduction: Along with allowing students to develop speed and agility, this game also introduces an element of strategy and cooperation.

Equipment: None

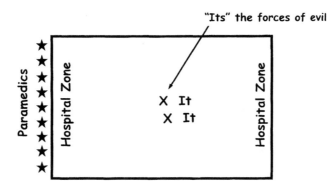

"Its" the forces of evil

Paramedics
★★★★★★★★★★

Hospital Zone

X It
X It

Hospital Zone

Game preparation: Designate a playing area, and mark off lines on opposing ends of the area. These lines are the Hospital Zone. Choose two students to be "it." They represent the Forces of Evil and stand in the middle of the playing area. The other students are the "Paramedics" and they line up on one of the Hospital Zone lines.

Game play: The "its" call "Emergency," which signals everyone to run to the opposite end line. The "its" try to tag as many "Paramedics" as possible before they reach the opposite end line. Paramedics who are tagged are "injured" and must freeze in place. Paramedics are safe when they are on either of the end lines. The game is non-stop with paramedics crossing the playing area in both directions at will as the "its" try to freeze everyone.

In order for an injured paramedic to be rescued, four other paramedics must go to the injured player and touch him or her all at one time, while still avoiding being tagged. Once four paramedics are touching an injured player, they are safe and are allowed to carry or drag the injured player to the Hospital Zone without being tagged. Once an injured player has reached the hospital zone, he or she can re-enter the game.

Tip:

- After two or three minutes, change the "its" and start the game over.

41. TOUCHDOWN

Introduction: This game requires speed, agility, as well as strategic planning.

Equipment:

- coins to use for objects to carry

Game preparation: Designate a large playing area and mark off two goal lines on opposing sides. Divide players into two teams—the Offense and the Defense—and have each team stand along one of the goal lines.

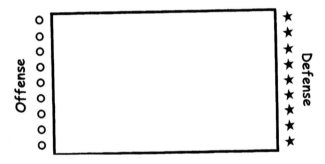

Game play: Secretly give the two or three players from the Offense coins to carry. The Offense goes into a huddle to decide which students are going to carry each of the coins. When you call out "Go," the offensive team must break the huddle and run toward the goal line being defended by the other team (the defense). All of the offensive players should hold their hands clenched in a fist as if they are carrying one of the objects.

The defenders run forward and tag as many offensive players as possible. An offensive player who gets tagged must immediately open both hands. Play continues until all of the players carrying objects are caught or they score touchdowns. Each touchdown scores six points.

When all of the coins have been discovered or safely taken to the other side, the roles of the teams are reversed. Teams keep taking turns until time is up. The team with the most points when the game ends wins.

Tips:

- This game can be played indoors or outdoors, but playing outdoors allows for a larger playing area and may be best for older players.

42. BOUNDARY BALL

Introduction: This is a very simple game that allows for full participation by all players. It is the reverse of dodge ball because the players roll the ball to areas where players from the opposing team are not positioned.

Equipment:

- two to eight rubber balls
- one long rope

Game preparation: Divide the gym or playing area into two equal sized courts. Separate the playing areas with a rope mounted no more than two feet off the ground. Divide the players into two teams and assign one team to each court. Each team gets a rubber ball.

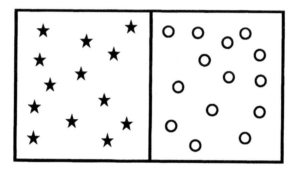

Game play: On the signal "go," each team attempts to roll their ball across the opponent's goal line. A team scores one point for each ball that makes it across. All balls must go under the rope or they do not count. To prevent balls from crossing their goal line, players can try and stop the ball in any manner possible. Add balls as the players demonstrate understanding of the rules.

The game continues without interruption for a set period of time or until a team scores a set number of points.

Tips:

- The game could be played with sponge balls, in which case the balls could be kicked instead of rolled.
- For a faster-paced game, start each team off with more than one ball and add balls as students learn the game.

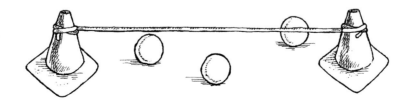

Section 5

TAG GAMES

Tag games have been around as long as children have played games. Because tag games keep everyone involved and active, the emphasis on winning and losing is greatly diminished and, generally, none of the players are singled out for not doing well. This makes tag games an excellent choice for any physical education class.

Tag games require a greater degree of strategy than other games covered so far in this book. Players need to make more decisions regarding where to move and how to move safely. This is because in these games, there is no defined movement pattern or area in which to move. In tag games, players are moving at all times in all directions.

Most of the tag games included in this chapter are short. They make great quick games for ending lessons or reviewing spatial awareness skills at any time during a lesson. The games have been organized according to their similarities and then listed in an order of progression from easier to more difficult.

Some guidelines for making tag games more exciting are:

- Use more than one "it." A good rule of thumb is to use one "it" for every five people playing. Round down if you are not sure how many "its" to use.

- Always identify the "its" with vests, arm bands, etc.

- If the game calls for the "its" changing roles when a tag is made, the "its" can carry an object like a ball for identification. After the tag is made, the ball is also exchanged. This is a good way for players to keep track of who's "it."

43. BUSY BEE TAG

Introduction: This activity reinforces students' spatial awareness skills and their coordination (and provides a few laughs).

Equipment: None

Game preparation: None

Game play: When you call the signal "Busy Bee," all of the players are to move in general space. As players are moving, call out various directions, such as "back to back," "knee to foot," etc. In response to the body part you call out, players are to pair up with the person closest to them and touch those body parts together. Let the children hold their positions for a few seconds and then call Busy Bee and repeat the process.

Tips:

- Allow the players to use their creativity to accomplish the task you call out. You will see a variety of correct responses.

- Play the game using the scientific names of bones and muscles with the older players.

- It is also possible to use this game in the classroom.

44. EVERYONE "IT" TAG

Grades 1–6

Objective: This is an excellent game to use while the students are learning spatial awareness skills.

Equipment: None

Game preparation: The game is played in a gymnasium, with no boundaries.

Game play: Players scatter throughout the playing area, with every player being "it." When you call out the start signal, everyone tries to tag as many players as possible, while avoiding being tagged. This point needs to be emphasized with young players. All players should count the number of tags they make. Stop the game after about one minute and let the children tell how many tags they made. No penalty for getting tagged. You just keep moving and count the tags you make.

Tips:

- Use different locomotor skills to change the speed of the game.

- You can require players to slide the first time they play the game. This will slow them down and avoid collisions.

- Always caution children about playing safely and avoiding collisions with others.

- It is better to play the game 3 or 4 times in short intervals rather than to try and play 4 or 5 minutes in a row.

45. FIRST AID TAG

Grades 1–6

Introduction: This game is a natural follow-up to "Everyone "It" and teaches one of the steps of first aid: applying direct pressure to a wound.

Equipment: None

Game preparation: None

Game play: Players scatter throughout the playing area, with every player being "it." When you call out the start signal, everyone tries to tag as many players as possible, while avoiding being tagged. When a person is tagged, he or she must apply first aid by holding the spot where he or she was tagged with one hand. The second time a player gets tagged, he or she grabs that spot with the other hand.

Players who have been tagged keep playing until they have been tagged three times. After the third tag, players must sit on the floor or leave the game until the game ends, because they now have no more hands for applying first aid.

Tips:

- Continue the game until about five players remain or a predetermined time limit is up.

- Use different locomotor skills to control the speed of the game.

46. FIRE TAG

Grades 2–6

Introduction: Along with enhancing students' spatial awareness skills, this game provides an opportunity to reinforce the fire safety rule of stop, drop, and roll. This is also a good way to practice falling safely.

Equipment: None

STOP!   DROP!   ROLL!

Game preparation: None

Game play: As with Everyone It and First Aid Tag, everyone is "it" in this game, and all players must try to tag as many other players as they can. Players who are tagged must stop, drop, and roll before they are free to continue tagging other players. Players must keep track of how many times they are tagged. After being tagged three times, a player has to sit cross-legged in the spot where she finished the third stop, drop, and roll.

Tips:

- Games only last about one minute so no one is eliminated for any length of time.

- It is better to play the game three or four times in short intervals rather than to try and play for four or five minutes in a row.

- Teach players what it means to stop, drop, and roll in a fire and why it's so important. Show them how to do it correctly so they can execute that skill on the floor safely.

47.   ZAPPED TAG

Grades 1–6

Introduction: Players in this game must avoid being tagged by the Zappers.

Equipment:

- 4–6 balls (or other object) for the "its" to carry

Game preparation: Choose five players to be "its" or Zappers. Each Zapper carries a sponge ball for identification.

Game play: Zappers can tag other players by touching them with the sponge ball, but they can never throw the ball.

Players who have been zapped become "its," but instead of chasing after other players, they must stand at the spot where they were zapped for the remainder of the game and try to tag players by reaching them without moving from that spot. (They can move one foot as long as the other foot remains firmly in place.)

Tip:

- A set of Zappers should only be allowed to be "it" for two minutes or less, regardless of how many people they have zapped.

48. ALIEN'S RAID TAG

Introduction: This is another basic tag game, but now the tags are made by stealing flags. There is an added element of mystery involved about getting back into the game after losing your flag.

Equipment:

- 1 flag for very player in the game (numbered flags work best)

Game preparation: Designate a playing area and place a circle the size of a hoop at each end of the playing area.

Game play: Give each player a flag to tuck into his or her belt. Remind players that they must be able to identify their own flags.

Players scatter throughout the playing area.

On the start signal all players try to steal as many flags from other players as possible. A stolen flag must be placed in one of the hoops before the player who stole it can go after another flag. A player whose flag has been stolen must immediately go to the sideline of the playing area and try to locate his or her flag. Upon doing so, the player can go grab it and get back in the game.

Players may have their own flag stolen while they are on the way to a hoop with a stolen flag, in which case they would first put the flag they have stolen into a circle and then go to the sidelines and look for their own flag.

Tip:

- Set a time limit prior to starting the game. Players who haven't had their flags stolen are the winners.

TAG GAMES with BASES

Grades 2–6

Traditional tag games have an "it" whose job is to touch someone else so that the "it" position is transferred to the person tagged. In another form of traditional tag, the pursued players may use various methods of being safe. This page, gives the following examples of these tag games:

Wood Tag: players are safe when touching wood.

Squat Tag: players are safe when squatting.

Line Tag: players are safe when standing on a line.

Skunk Tag: players are safe when holding one hand under one leg and squeezing their nose with the same hand.

Turkish Tag: players are safe when standing on one foot and crossing their arms like a Turkish Sultan.

When playing tag games of this type, impose a limit on how long players may stay in the safe position or how many times they can use a safe position during the game. Also, sometimes you may consider using more than one "it" for a more active game. When playing with multiple "its," the "its" should carry a ball or some type of identification that is easily exchanged. A good rule of thumb is to have one "it" for every five people playing.

49.   BALANCE TAG

Grades 2–6

Introduction: This is a basic tag game that allows students the opportunity to create balancing positions quickly.

Equipment:

- Nerf balls (one for every five players)

Game preparation: Assign one "it" for every five players and give each "it" a nerf ball for identification.

Game play: The "its" chase and tag the other players. When a player is tagged, that player becomes "it" and takes the nerf ball from the player who made the tag.

Players can balance on three or four body parts to be safe. If they lose their balance, they can be tagged.

Tips:

- Play short games (1 or 2 minutes), and switch "its" after each game.
- Set a time limit on how long a person can stay in the safe position.

50. HIP TUNNEL TAG

Introduction: This game gets its name from the position players must hold to indicate they have been caught and are waiting to be freed. This game sometimes is called Frozen Tag or Chinese Tag. It is sort of the grand daddy of tag games.

Equipment:

- identification items for the "its" (vests, arm bands, etc.)

Game preparation: Select one "it" for every five players and identify each with a vest (or some other form of identification).

Game play: The remaining players take a scattered position within the playing area. As the game starts, the "its" begin chasing and tagging players. Players who are caught must freeze and stand with their legs apart and their hands on their hips. Players who have not been caught can unfreeze the frozen players by crawling through their legs.

Tips:

- Free players need to be encouraged to free frozen players.
- Play either until the "its" have frozen everyone or for a two- to three-minute time period, then pick new "its" and start a new game. (Playing longer than three minutes is not advisable because the "its" will get too tired.)

51. BRIDGE TRAPPING TAG

Introduction: This game is a modification of Hip Tunnel Tag, but it allows frozen players to be more creative. This is an excellent game to play after working with bridges in a movement theme.

Equipment:

- identification items for the "its" (vests, arm bands, etc.)

Game preparation: Select one "it" for every five players and identify each with a vest (or some other form of identification).

Game play: This game is played the same way as Hip Tunnel Tag, except that players who are tagged must make a bridge with their body (by holding a position on their feet and hands, for example). Any bridge is acceptable as long as three or more body parts are used for support and another player can crawl under it. When another player can crawl under a frozen player's bridge, the frozen player is back in the game.

Tips:

- Free players need to be encouraged to free frozen players.
- Play either until the "its" have frozen everyone or for a two- to three-minute time period, then pick new "its" and start a new game. (Playing longer than three minutes is not advisable because the "its" will get too tired.)

52. HIT THE DECK TAG

Introduction: "Hit the Deck" is an old war cry given for protection. That still holds, if you can "Hit the Deck" in this game you will be safe.

Equipment:

- identification items for the "its" (vests, arm bands, etc.)

Game preparation: Select one "it" for every five players and identify each with a vest (or some other form of identification).

Game play: The remaining players take a scattered position within the playing area. As the game starts, the "its" begin chasing and tagging players. Players who are caught lie down on their stomachs. Free players can unfreeze tagged players (players lying on their stomachs) by patting them on the back three times.

A player may "hit the deck" any time to be safe and avoid being tagged. But when they hit the deck to be safe, players must immediately roll onto their back and hold their arms and legs up in the air and shake them. This position is called the "Dying Cockroach." Players can stay in the "Dying Cockroach" position for a maximum of five seconds. An "it" may stand near a player in this position, count the 5 seconds and tag the runner before he or she can run away.

Tips:

- Play either until the "its" have frozen everyone or for a two- to three-minute time period, then pick new "its" and start a new game. (Playing longer than three minutes is not advisable because the "its" will get too tired.)

53.   FUNNY FACE TAG

Grades 2–4

Introduction: This game has an element of humor because everyone will be making funny faces.

Equipment:

- identification items for the "its" (vests, arm bands, etc.)

Game preparation: Select one "it" for every five players and identify each with a vest or some other form of identification.

Game play: The remaining players take a scattered position within the playing area. If an "it" touches another player, that player must freeze in that spot and make a funny face, freezing in that position.

Players who are still free can unfreeze a frozen player by stopping in front of him or her, making a funny face back at the frozen player and counting to three out loud. When those three steps have been completed, the frozen player is freed and back in the game.

Tips:

- Play either until the "its" have frozen everyone or for a two- to three-minute time period, then pick new "its" and start a new game. (Playing longer than three minutes is not advisable because the "its" will get too tired.)

54. BARNYARD TAG

Introduction: This is a basic tag game that allows the students to have fun with sound effects.

Equipment:

- identification items for the "its" (vests, arm bands, etc.)

Game preparation: Select one "it" for every five players and have each wear a vest for identification.

Game play: The "its" are farmers, and the rest of the players are barnyard animals. Have the barnyard animals scatter throughout the playing area.

When a farmer tags an animal, the farmer gives that player the name of an animal. The tagged player freezes in a position that resembles the assigned animal and makes the sound of that animal. To free a frozen animal, a player who has not been caught must face the frozen animal and make that animal's sound three times. A free player who is tagged while trying to free a frozen one will also become frozen.

Tips:

- Play either until the "its" have frozen everyone or for a two- to three-minute time period, then pick new "its" and start a new game. (Playing longer than three minutes is not advisable because the "its" will get too tired.)

55.   ART GALLERY TAG

Grades 3–6th

Introduction: This is a variation on the basic tag game but it contains an unique method of setting frozen players free.

Equipment:

- identification items for the "its" (vests, arm bands, etc.)

Game preparation: Select one "it" for every five players and have each wear a vest or use some other form of identification.

Game play: The "its" are caretakers of the art gallery, and the rest of the players are art lovers. Have the art lovers scatter throughout the playing area. The art lovers must try to avoid being tagged. Those who are tagged must assume the pose of a hideous statue. A statue can become unfrozen if two free players can join hands and encircle the statue and count to three out loud. If a player is tagged while saving another player, the entire trio is turned into statues. They drop hands and make individual statues.

Tips:

- Play either until the "its" have frozen everyone or for a two- to three-minute time period, then pick new "its" and start a new game. (Playing longer than three minutes is not advisable because the "its" may get too tired.)

56. INTERNET TAG

Introduction: This game adds a new level of strategy to tag, because the players being chased have a method to fight back and capture the "its."

Equipment:

- identification items for the "its" (vests, arm bands, etc.)

Game preparation: Select one "it"—or computer virus—for every five players and have each wear a vest (or use some other form of identification).

Game play: The computer viruses must try to tag the other players. A player tagged by a virus is frozen and considered "contaminated." The only way to free a contaminated player is for two non-contaminated players to encircle the frozen player and yell "On Line."

If four non-contaminated players can surround a virus in a circle with their hands held and yell "de-bugged" three times, that virus, or "it," is eliminated and becomes one of the non-contaminated players. If the players can de-bug all of the viruses, the players win. If the viruses can contaminate everyone, the viruses win. Players who are circling a virus can still be contaminated. It is very difficult to capture a virus.

Tips:

- Play either until the viruses have contaminated everyone or for a three- to four-minute time period, then pick new viruses and start a new game. (Playing longer than three minutes is not advisable because the "its" may get too tired.)

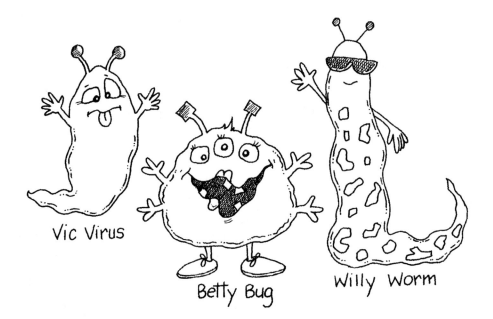

Vic Virus

Betty Bug

Willy Worm

57. LEAPFROG TAG

Introduction: This is a basic tag game that incorporates jumping and leaping skills.

Equipment:

- identification items for the "its" (vests, arm bands, etc.)

Game preparation: Select one "it" (frog catcher) for every five players (frogs). Have each frog catcher wear a vest or use some other method of identification.

Game play: Have the frogs scatter throughout the playing area.

When you give the signal, the frog catchers chase and tag the frogs. When a frog is tagged, the frog freezes in the frog-position (squatting, hands on the floor for stability, arms straight, shoulders up, head tucked). Frozen frogs can be set free by having another frog leapfrog over them.

Tips:

- It is important that correct leapfrog form be taught prior to playing the game.
- Play until the "its" have frozen everyone or play for a two- to three-minute time period, then pick new frog catchers.

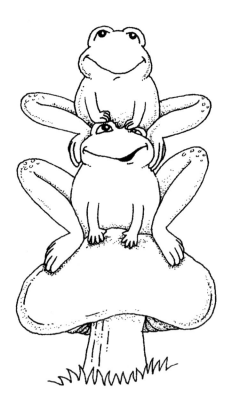

58. MATH FACTS TAG

Grades 3–6

Introduction: This tag game allows for the integration of math into a physical education activity.

Equipment:

- identification items for the "its" (vests, arm bands, etc.)

Game preparation: Select one "it" for every five players and identify each with a vest or some other form of identification.

Game play: The remaining players take a scattered position within the playing area. As the game starts, the "its" begin chasing and tagging players. Players who are caught must assume the dying cockroach position (lying on their backs and holding their arms and legs up in the air and shaking them). Tagged players can be freed when a free player comes up to them and gives them a math fact of a type specified by the teacher (addition, multiplication, etc.). If the frozen player answers correctly he or she is back in the game.

Tips:

- Play until the "its" have frozen everyone or for a two- to three-minute time period, then pick new "its" and repeat the game. (Playing longer than three minutes is not advisable because the "its" may get too tired.)

$$3 \times 7 = ?$$

$$? \times 3 = 15$$

$$2 \times ? = 6$$

59. SPELLING TAG

Grades 3–6

Introduction: This tag game allows for the integration of spelling into a physical education activity.

Equipment:

- identification items for the "its" (vests, arm bands, etc.)

Game preparation: Select one "it" for every five players and identify each with a vest or some other form of identification.

Game play: The remaining players take a scattered position within the playing area. As the game starts, the "its" begin chasing and tagging players. Players who are caught must assume the dying cockroach position (lying on their backs and holding their arms and legs up in the air and shaking them). Tagged players can be freed when a free player comes up to them and gives them a word to spell (preferably from a designated list). If the frozen player spells the word correctly he or she is back in the game.

Tips:

- This is a good time to use the student's weekly spelling list.

- Play until the "its" have frozen everyone or for a two- to three-minute time period, then pick new "its" and start a new game. (Playing longer than three minutes is not advisable because the "its" may get too tired.)

Spelling List

1. China
2. Europe
3. Japan
4. Australia
5. India
6. France

60. STATE CAPITOLS TAG

Grades 3–6

Introduction: This tag game allows for integration of social studies into a physical education activity.

Equipment:

- identification items for the "its" (vests, arm bands, etc.)

Game preparation: Select one "it" for every five players and identify each with a vest or some other form of identification.

Game play: The remaining players take a scattered position within the playing area. As the game starts, the "its" begin chasing and tagging players. Players who are caught must assume the dying cockroach position (lying on their backs and holding their arms and legs up in the air and shaking them). Tagged players can be freed when a free player gives them the name of a state and they correctly identify the capital.

Tips:

- It may be easier to limit the list of states players may use.
- Play until the "its" have frozen everyone or for a two- to three-minute time period, then pick new "its" and start a new game. (Playing longer than three minutes is not advisable because the "its" may get too tired.)

73

61. BEAN BAG FREEZE TAG

Grades 1–3

Introduction: This is a basic tag game that requires an element of cooperation.

Equipment:

- one beanbag per player
- an object for each "it" to carry, such as a nerf ball, deck ring, or yarn ball

Game preparation: Select one "it" for every five players in the game and give each "it" an identifying object to carry. Give each player, including the "its," a beanbag.

Game play: Have all players (including the "its") balance the bean bag on a body part you specify (shoulder, arm, back of hand, etc.). When you give the signal, the "its" must chase the other players and tag them with the object they are carrying. When a tag is made, the "it" gives the object to the tagged player, who now takes the player's place as "it." The new "it" needs to chase a new player and not try to retag the "it" that caught them.

Players who drop their bean bag become frozen until another player can pick up their beanbag and place it back on them. If an "it" drops their bean bag, only another "it" can pick up the bean bag and place it on them.

Tips:

- This can be a never-ending game. Play for a designated time period, then discuss some needed strategies to refine the game. Play again with new "its."

62. PAC MAN TAG

Grades 2–4

Introduction: This game is a take off on the video game of the same name.

Equipment:

- Identification vests of two different colors; three of one color, and one of another color

Game preparation: If the play area doesn't already have lines on it (as gymnasiums usually do), mark off lines going in different directions. Choose three players to be "it"—the Pac Men—and one player to be the ghost. Identify the three Pac Men with vests of the same color. Identify the ghost with a vest of a different color. The remaining players are the dots (as seen in the video game).

Game play: Every player in Pac Man must always move by following a line, including the "its." Players must use only the walking skill.

The Pac Men want to catch the dots. When a dot has been caught, that player leaves the game. The ghost's job is to catch the Pac Men. If a Pac Man is caught, they also leave the game.

Tips:

- The game ends when the ghost eliminates the three Pac Men or the Pac Men catch all of the dots.

- The game can also end at the end of a specified time limit (No longer then 5 minutes) or when only a few players remain

- To maximize participation, consider having players re-enter the game when the ghost catches the Pac Man who tagged them.

- Because this is a walking activity, it is a good game to use as a cool down at the end of a lesson. As players are eliminated from the game, they can get in line to be dismissed.

63. BATMAN AND ROBIN TAG

Grades 3–6

Introduction: A theme type game building on the popularity of the Batman movies and comics.

Equipment:

- 7 identification vests; 5 of one color, 2 of another

Game preparation: Depending on the number of players, select four or five to be Batman's enemies (the Joker, Catwoman, Mr. Freeze, the Penguin, etc.). Identify them with vests of one color. Select two players to be Batman (or Batgirl) and Robin and have them wear the vests of another color.

Game play: The remaining players scatter in the playing area and try to keep from being tagged by Batman's enemies. Players who are tagged by an enemy are frozen and must get down on their hands and knees. Batman and Robin may never be tagged by an enemy. Their job is to move around and unfreeze the frozen players by tagging them. Once they have been unfrozen, players may re-enter the game. If four or more players are frozen at the end of the designated playing time, Batman's enemies win; if there are three or less players frozen, Batman and Robin win.

Tips:

- A game should last no longer than two minutes. At the end of the two minutes, select new "its" and repeat the game.

64. NINJA TURTLE® TAG

Grades 3–6th

Introduction: This is a novelty game based on the Ninja Turtle® characters.

Equipment:

- pinnies or vests of different colors; 4 of one color and at least 2 of another color

Game preparation: Designate a four-sided playing area. (In a small gym use the entire playing space. In a large gym with an average sized class, use the volleyball court.) Choose four players to be Ninja Turtles. Have each wear a vest for identification and stand behind one of the boundary lines (sewers) of the playing area. Designate two or three players to be "its"—or "Shredders"—and have them wear the vests of the alternate color. Have the "Shredders" stand in the center of the playing area.

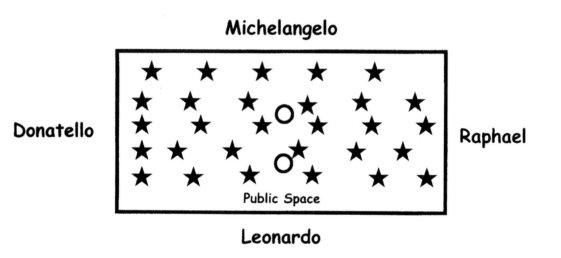

Game play: All remaining players must scatter throughout the area inside the public space—the playing space. The players inside the public space have to avoid being tagged by the "Shredders."

Players are safe from being tagged by a "Shredder" by assuming the "dying cockroach" position. (lying on their backs and putting arms and legs up in the air). Players can stay in that position for five seconds. After five seconds they must get up or they can be tagged lying down. Players who are tagged must lie down on their stomach and stay on the floor until a Ninja Turtle rescues them.

Ninja Turtles can rescue a tagged player by leaving their sewer area and dragging that player back to the sewer with them. Upon reaching the sewer, the Ninja Turtle and the rescued player shake hands and say "Cowabunga Dude." At that time the rescued player can re-enter the public space.

A Ninja Turtle is always safe while in the sewer. However, a Shredder can catch a Ninja Turtle who is out of the sewer. If a Ninja Turtle is tagged in the public space, the Ninja Turtle must lie down on their stomach and they may not be rescued.

The object of the game is for the "Shredders" to see if they can freeze everyone in the public space.

65. BLARNEY STONE TAG

Grades 3–6

Introduction: This theme tag game is great for St. Patrick's Day.

Equipment:

- 5 hoops

- 1 large paper shamrock for each "it" to carry

Game preparation: Select one "Leprechaun"—or "it"—for every five players and have each carry a shamrock for identification. Scatter the hoops throughout the playing area to represent Blarney Stones.

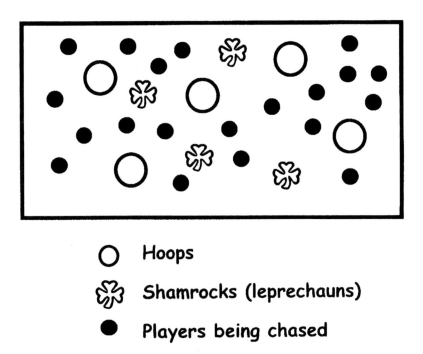

◯	**Hoops**
✿	**Shamrocks (leprechauns)**
●	**Players being chased**

Game play: The leprechauns chase the remaining players. When a leprechaun tags a player, that player gets the shamrock and takes the leprechaun's place as "it."

To be "safe," players may stand on a Blarney Stone and stay there until another player comes up to them and says, "Kiss the Blarney Stone." At that signal, the person on the Blarney Stone must leave the safe zone.

Tips:

- Play for two to three minutes and repeat the game.

66. SQUEEZE AND SING TAG

Grades 4–6

Introduction: Start this game by having the class sing a chorus of "Row, Row, Row Your Boat." Then have them try singing the chorus in one breath. If they think this is hard, warn them how hard it will be after they have been running because this is how they get to be safe in this game.

Equipment:

- 1 Nerf ball for every "it."

Game preparation: Select one "it" for every five players, and give each one of the "its" a ball to carry.

Game play: The remaining players scatter around the playing area and the "its" try to tag them. Players who get tagged get the ball from the "it" who tagged them, and they in turn become new "its" and try to tag other players. The purpose of carrying the balls is merely for identification. The "its" may not throw the ball to tag players.

Players can be safe by pairing up with a partner, holding both hands and squeezing, and singing "Row, Row, Row Your Boat," but only for as long as they can sing on one breath. When one of the partners takes a breath or stops singing both players must take off to find new partners to squeeze and sing with in order to be safe. This is a very fast-moving game with lots of singing and laughing.

Tips:

- Change the safety rule from pairing up in twos to holding hands and singing in groups of three.

- Try having players whistle the tune to be safe, instead of singing.

67.   FLAG TAG

Introduction: This game allows for review of some ball skills in a game situation. A basketball dribble works best. (See Section 10 for another version of this game that is played without a ball.) .

Equipment:

- 1 flag per player
- 1 ball per player (basketball or similar-sized ball works best)

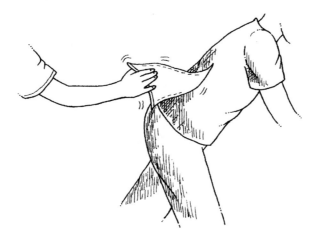

Game preparation: Players position their flags in the middle of their backsides, holding it in place with their belt or the elastic of their pant waists. Players then scatter in the playing area, each carrying a ball.

Game play: On the start signal, all players begin dribbling and moving throughout the playing area, trying to steal as many flags as possible while dribbling their ball under control. Players carry their stolen flags in one hand. A player whose flag has been stolen is not eliminated from the game, and can keep dribbling and stealing flags.

At the end of a one- or two-minute time limit, players who still have their own flags receive a bonus. When you call a halt to the action, each player totals up the flags he or she has stolen and gets one point for each, and adds to that any bonus points. The players with the highest totals win the game.

Tips:

- Designate the point value of the bonus before each round. Vary the amount of the bonus.
- Use an elimination process. Players whose flag is stolen are out of the game.
- When a player's flag is stolen, have that player leave the game and pay some type of a quick penalty (such as dribble the ball ten times through their legs) to return to the game.

68. HOOP SCOOT TAG

Introduction: This is a tag game that incorporates an element of strategy.

Equipment:

- five–nine hoops
- three–five Nerf balls

Game preparation: Scatter the hoops in the play area, several feet apart. Select players to be "it" and give each of them a nerf ball to carry for identification. The remaining players must stand inside one of the hoops, but no more than three players inside one hoop at any time.

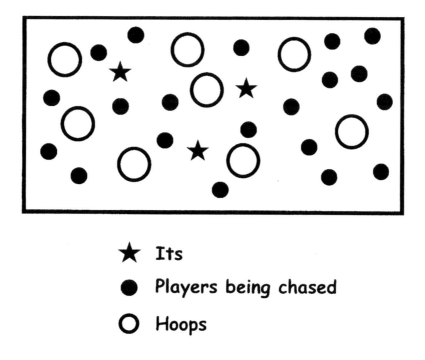

★ **Its**

● **Players being chased**

O **Hoops**

Game play: The objective is for players to run from one hoop to another without being tagged by an "it." No one is allowed to remain in a hoop for more than five seconds. If a player stays too long in a hoop an "it" can count the seconds and, if after five seconds the player hasn't left the hoop, he or she is caught automatically. When an "it" tags a player the two switch roles and the nerf ball gets passed to the new "it," and the game continues.

Tips:

- Play for two to three minutes and repeat the game.

69. COWBOY TAG

Introduction: A discussion of the importance of the horse to the cowboy can serve as an introduction to the importance of cooperation between partners in this game.

Equipment: None

Game preparation: Designate a playing area to be the range, and in one corner of the range set up a small area that will serve as the corral. The range is where the cattle will run, and the corral is where the players (cattle) go after they have been tagged. Choose two children to be the first cowboy.

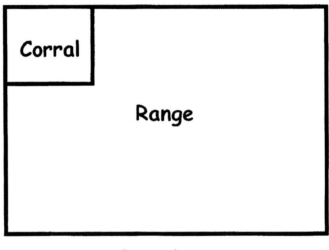

Boundary

Game play: The two children who are the cowboy (or cowgirl) join hands and work as a team (horse and rider) tagging the cattle and bringing them to the corral. The two must hold hands at all times and tag only one player (cow) at a time. After tagging a person, the "cowboy"—or "it"— must encircle (lasso) the person and immediately bring him or her to the corral. As soon as two children are tagged and corralled, they join hands and become another cowboy and corral other players. This continues until all but a handful of children are cowboys. Two of the remaining players could be chosen to start a new game.

Tips:

- Because it may be unsafe for a large group to be chasing just a few players, it may be wise to end the game when there are about five cows left.

- As in the other tag games monitor the "its" for tiredness.

70. WASP TAG

Introduction: This game is played entirely with a partner and allows students to experience the cooperation necessary to move strategically with a partner to escape being tagged, to make a tag, and to move safely at all times.

Equipment:

- 3 (7- to 8-inch) nerf balls

Game preparation: All players must pair up with a partner and hold hands. Choose three couples to be "wasps"—or "its"—and give each of the wasps a Nerf ball to carry, which will be their stinger. Have the players scatter throughout the playing area.

Game play: On the "go" signal, all of the couples are free to move, but partners must hold hands throughout the game. The wasps must attempt to "sting" (tag) another couple by touching them with the nerf ball. When a sting is made the wasps pass the nerf ball to the stung couple, who are now the new wasps.

Tips:

- Play the game for 2 minutes or less, then have everyone select a new partner and repeat the game.

- These directions are for a group of twenty-five to thirty players. If playing with a smaller group, you may need to start with one or two wasps instead of three.

71. LOOSE CABOOSE TAG

Grades 3–5

Introduction: A reminder that every complete train has an engine and a caboose is a good way to introduce Loose Caboose.

Equipment: None

Game preparation: Organize players into groups of three or four and have players in each group stand one behind the other with their hands on the hips of the person in front of them. (This represents a train.)

Select 3–4 players (for a class of 25 or so) to be "its." The "its" represent the "loose cabooses," because they aren't connected to a "train."

Game play: The trains are free to move around the playing area at will, as long as their train does not break. The "Loose Cabooses" try and attach themselves to the end of a train. When a caboose becomes attached to a train, that train yells "Loose Caboose" and then the front person leaves the group and become a loose caboose.

Tips:

- If the playing area is too large the "loose cabooses" will have a difficult time catching on to a train, thus a smaller playing area usually makes for a better game.

- Play for 2 to 3 minutes, then have the players talk about strategy and repeat the game.

72. ALLIGATOR'S TAIL TAG

Grades 3–6

Introduction: Tell the children that they are going to be like a great alligator in the swamp who doesn't like anyone to touch its tail.

Equipment:

- scarfs or flags to use for the alligators' tails (one for each alligator)

Game preparation: Organize the players in groups of nine or ten players, and have each group form a line. Everyone in the line must hold the waist of the person in front of them. The last person in the line tucks a "tail" in the back of their belt.

Game play: When you give the signal, the first person in line—the head of the alligator—start to chase the tail. The players in the line have to work together to try and prevent the head from catching the tail, while making sure their line doesn't break. If the head catches the tail, the head becomes the tail and the second person in line becomes the new head.

Tip:

- This is a great game, but it should be played for only a short period of time, as the children will tire rapidly.

73. ADDITION TAG

Introduction: For younger players, a review of the fundamental mathematics facts such as 1+1=2, 2+1=3, and 2+2=4 can provide the background to lead into Addition Tag.

Equipment: None

Game preparation: Scatter the players within the playing area and select two people to be "it." These two players must join hands and cannot let go.

Game play: The "its" job is to tag one of the other players, who then joins their line. The three players who are "it" continue to try to tag other players. When four players make up the "it" line, the line is divided in half, and there are now two "its." Play continues in like manner until everyone has been caught.

Tips:

- It is sometimes difficult for the first "it" to catch two more players to make a new "it." The game will move faster if you choose two couples to be "it" instead of one.

- Monitor the game to make sure players who are "it" do not get too tired.

74. AMOEBA TAG

Introduction: This game is a spin-off of Addition Tag. A good lead-in is to discuss the organism called the amoeba and that it reproduces by dividing in half to make a new cell.

Equipment: None

Game preparation: Choose three players to be the first Amoeba. To make the Amoeba, the three players join hands. All other players scatter throughout the playing area.

Game play: Working as a team, the Amoeba must try to catch the remaining players. As the Amoeba catches a player, that person joins the Amoeba and joins hands with the person in the Amoeba who made the tag. Now the Amoeba is made up of four players. The Amoeba keeps catching players and when "it" (Amoeba) has grown to six players, it divides in the middle to form two Amoebas. The game continues until all players have been caught and are part of an Amoeba or until a handful of players still have not been caught.

Tips:

- Depending on the number of players, try starting the game with two Amoebas instead of one.

- Monitor the game to make sure players who are "it" do not get too tired.

75. GLOBOID TAG

Introduction: Because the Globoid is a demon from the deep that will devour all living things, this game is an all-time favorite of children ages eight to twelve. It's helpful if children have played games such as Addition Tag or Amoeba Tag prior to playing this game (see pages 86 and 87).

Equipment: None

Game preparation: Choose one player to be "it" or the "globoid."

Game play: The globoid's goal is to keep growing by tagging as many players as possible. As soon as the globoid tags a player, that player becomes part of the "it" by holding the hand of the person who made the tag. Only the ends of the Globoid can make tags. The pursued players may not go through the Globoid by ducking under held hands or by trying to break through the line. The Globoid's goal is to get everyone into the Globoid Line. Any player who runs outside of the playing area boundary to escape the Globoid is automatically caught and joins the end of the line.

Tips:

- Be careful not to let the boundaries get too large.

- To be successful the Globoid line needs to learn to let the middle of the line lead and not to follow one of the end people. Sometimes it is helpful if you begin as the "it" and help the players learn to let the middle of the line lead.

76. DOUBLE GLOBOID TAG

Grades 3–6

Introduction: This game is played exactly like Globoid Tag (see page 88) except that it starts with two Globoids, which makes it more difficult for players to keep from getting caught.

Equipment: None

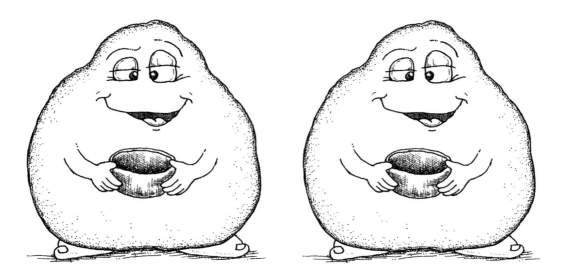

Game preparation: Choose two players to be two separate "its," or "Globoids."

Game play: Each Globoid's goal is to keep growing by tagging as many players as possible. As soon as the Globoid tags a player, that player becomes part of the "it" by holding the hand of the person who made the tag. Only the ends of the Globoid can make tags. The pursued players may not go through the Globoid by ducking under held hands or by trying to break through the line. Any player who runs outside of the playing area boundary to escape the Globoid is automatically caught and joins the end of the Globoid that was in pursuit.

Tips:

- Children usually do not think about having the two Globoids work together to catch fleeing players. After playing a turn or two, talk to players about how they might be more effective at tagging players if the Globoids cooperated. The game gets better when they finally understand this strategy.

- Playing Globoid Tag before playing Double Globoid Tag will make it easier for children to play this game.

77. PIRATES' GOLD TAG

Grades 2–5

Introduction: Students don't seem to be familiar with pirates in these days of Star Wars warriors, but after a brief discussion of what pirates were, the students get into an enthusiastic mood to steal the treasure.

Equipment:

- 13 bean bags (pieces of gold)

Game preparation: Mark off a 12′ × 12′ area in the center of the playing space to represent the Pirate's Island. Place the thirteen bean bags (bags of gold) in the center of the island. Choose one player to be the first pirate, and have that player stand in the center of the island. The rest of the players must stand around the perimeter of the island, but out of arms reach of the pirate.

Game play: The players begin walking around the island. When the pirate says "Pirates Gold" the players can begin trying to steal the gold off the island, but must avoid being tagged by the Pirate.

A player may be tagged whether they have gold or not. Any player who is tagged is out of the game and must give back any gold he or she has stolen. The Pirate can never step off the island but can tag any players within reach, even if they are not on the island.

The game is over when there is only one player left with at least one bag of gold in his or her possession or when all the gold has been stolen, in which case the player with the most gold would be the winner.

Tips:

- To keep the game more active and more players involved, establish a rule for how players can re-enter the game. For example, you might allow two players to re-enter the game (on a first-out, first-in basis) every time a bag of gold is successfully stolen.

- It can be very difficult for one player to defend the gold, so consider starting out with two pirates to make the game more interesting.

- Emphasize the importance of honesty in regards to being tagged and leaving the game with out being told they were tagged.

78. TEMPLE OF DOOM TAG

Grades 4–6

Introduction: This is an advanced version of Pirate's Gold Tag (see page 90) and is based on the movie about Indiana Jones exploring the Temple of Doom.

Equipment:

- 13 plastic bowling pins to be used for the treasure,

- several large objects to be used for constructing the maze (folding mats set on edge work well). All obstacles used for the maze need to project into the air to make pretend chambers and hallways. Be creative.

Game preparation: Construct a maze similar to the one shown in the diagram. This maze is the Temple of Doom. Designate an area outside the temple to serve as the museum. Place the treasure in the middle of the temple, and select one or two players to be the temple guards. Have the remaining players scatter around the outside of the temple's boundary.

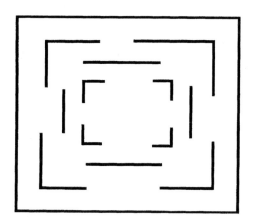

Game play: The players must attempt to steal the treasure. Players can steal as many pieces of treasure as they can carry. Once a person has stolen a piece of treasure, he or she must place it in the museum and go back for more.

Players may move in and out of the temple at random. Players may be caught whether they are carrying treasure or not. Players who are caught must retire from the game and return any treasure in their possession. The temple guards may never leave the boundary of the temple to pursue players.

Tips:

- To keep more players involved in the game, establish a rule for how players can re-enter the game. For example, you might allow two players to re-enter the game (on a first-out, first-in basis) every time a treasure is successfully stolen.

- Depending on the skills of the group, it may make for a more challenging and exciting game if there are more than two guards; however, four should be the maximum number of guards.

Section 6

SCATTER FORMATION GAMES

Scatter games get their classification because the activities do not have consistent starting formations. Also, the participants have a lot of freedom regarding where they move, how they move, and why they might move.

Most of the games in this section involve a lot of activity and vigorous exercise. However, a few are slower and work well as cool down activities, ice breakers, and cooperative challenges.

The order of progression for these games is not as important as in the other sections. For that reason the games are organized by similarities, not according to their level of difficulty.

79. WHISTLE MIXER

Grades K–6

Introduction: This activity can be used as either a game or as a class management tool.

Equipment:

- a whistle
- drum,
- or tambourine

Game preparation: Have the players scatter throughout the play area. Assign different instructions to every number of whistle-blows. For example, one blow may mean everyone must freeze, two blows mean students have five seconds to find a partner, three blows mean students must get into groups of three, and so forth.

Game play: When you give the start signal, all players begin moving in all directions in the play area. After the players move for ten to fifteen seconds, blow the whistle. When everyone has properly responded to the whistle signal (for example, found a partner in response to the two-whistle-blast signal), repeat the procedure, using a different signal (number of whistle blows) each time.

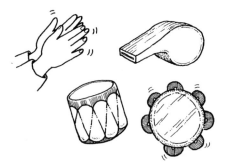

Tips:

- It is best to limit the number of whistle blows to five, because beyond that children may have a difficult time keeping track of the number of whistles as well as their designated meaning.

- Give the children who do not properly respond to the signal a one-point penalty. Whenever a player earns three points, he or she has to perform a humorous but slightly unpleasant penalty on the sideline. As soon as the penalty is completed the student can rejoin the game.

- If this is being used as a class management tool for grouping students for an activity, students not able to get into the proper-sized group within the specified time limit can report to the teacher, who will then assign them to a group.

- Try using a drum, tambourine, or clapping your hands as a way of giving signals.

- Assign different locomotor skills—such as skipping, jumping, or hopping on one foot—that children must use to complete the designated task.

80. KNOCK'EM DOWN AND SET'EM UP

Grades 1–3

Introduction: This activity is adaptable to several situations. Although only half of the group is active at a time, the rotation of the teams moves rapidly so the waiting times are short.

Equipment:

- 25 to 30 bowling pins (or other objects that can be knocked down and set up again—for example, cones, liter soda pop bottles, etc.)
- a stop watch

Game preparation: Divide the class into two groups and line them up on opposite sidelines of the playing area. Set up the bowling pins in random positions throughout the playing area.

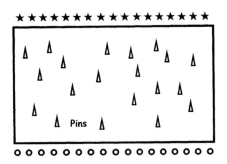

Game play: Give the start signal and start the time as one team races into the playing area and knocks down every object using only their hands. When all the objects are knocked down the players must run back to the starting line and sit down. Once everyone is seated, give the "go" signal again. This time the team must run back into the playing area and begin setting up all of the objects. When all of the objects are standing, players return to the starting line and sit down. When the last player sits down, stop the timer.

Either record the score or just call it out, then have the other team repeat the process. The team with the fastest time wins that round.

Tips:

- Play two or three rounds and designate the team with the lowest total time as the winner. This is also more fun because as children get the hang of the game, they can complete the tasks in a shorter time.
- For a variation on this game, try having players dribble a ball soccer style and use the ball to knock over the pins. When all of the pins are down, the players can dribble their balls back to the starting line. When all of the players are sitting, they leave their balls on the line and run out to set up the pins. The remainder of the game is the same.
- Try having players dribble a ball basketball style. Now they need to knock the pins down with their hands while still controlling their ball. They must also dribble the ball while setting up the pins.

81. CLEANNIES AND MESSIES

Introduction: This is a great activity to use either as a quick hitter at the beginning of a physical education lesson or as a game by itself.

Equipment:

- 12 or more cones

Game preparation: Divide the class evenly into two teams: the Cleannies and the Messies. Place the cones randomly throughout the playing area, with all of them standing.

Game play: When you give the start signal, the Messies must try to knock over as many cones as they can and the Cleannies must set up as many cones as they can. At the end of 30 seconds, the group that has more cones in their desired position (standing or knocked over) is the winner. Change groups and repeat the game.

Tips:

- This game is high energy and the excitement will be high, but students will likely lose interest after playing three or four games; therefore, it's better to repeat the game on different days rather than play for too long on one day.

82. NUMBERS AND LETTERS

Grades 1–6

Introduction: This game is based on Cleannies and Messies (see page 97), but it uses more cones. The game especially helps very young primary school students quickly differentiate between numbers and letters.

Equipment:

18 or more cones

Game preparation: Mark half of the cones with a random number and the other half with a random letter. Place the cones standing up randomly throughout the playing area. Divide the class into two teams: the Numbers and the Letters.

Game play: When you give the start signal, the Numbers try to knock down the cones with letters on them and set up the cones with numbers on them. Conversely, the Letters try to knock down the cones with numbers on them and set up the cones with letters on them. Play for a thirty- to sixty-second time period, then declare the team with the most cones standing the winner.

Tips:

- Although this is a high-energy game, students will likely lose interest after playing three or four games; therefore, play the game two or three times and come back to it on another day.

83. CONSONANTS AND VOWELS

Introduction: This game is the same as Numbers and Letters (see page 98), but the cones are marked with either consonants or vowels. This is a good way to help young children reinforce their recognition of consonants and vowels.

Equipment:

• 18 or more cones (At least 18 cones for a class of 25.)

Game preparation: Mark half of the cones with a random consonant and the other half with a random vowel. Use y as a vowel in this game. Place the cones standing up randomly throughout the playing area. Divide the class into two teams: the Consonants and the Vowels.

Game play: When you give the start signal, the Consonants must try to knock down the cones with vowels on them and set up the cones with consonants on them. Conversely, the Vowels must try to knock down the cones with consonants on them and set up the cones with vowels on them. After playing for a thirty- to sixty-second time period, declare the team with the most cones standing the winner.

Tips:

• Although this is a high-energy game, students will likely lose interest after playing three or four games; therefore, play the game two or three times and come back to it on another day.

• This same idea could be applied to review several concepts, such as food groups and odds and even.

84. CONCENTRATION

Introduction: This is a novelty game based on the popular television game show Concentration. The game requires agility and, of course, concentration.

Equipment:

- a deck of playing cards

- poly spots (one per playing card being used)

Game preparation: Divide the class into teams of three and—starting at Ace and working down the deck order—assign a playing card label to each team—for example, the Aces, the Kings, the Queens, etc. Line the teams up as shown in the diagram. Using only the playing cards that have an assigned team, spread the cards on the floor face down as shown. (Each "?" represents a card.) Spread the cards out so they will take up a lot of space. To make the cards easier to see and to keep in one spot, lay each card on top of a poly spot.

★	★	★	★	★	★	★	★
★	★	★	★	★	★	★	★
★	★	★	★	★	★	★	★
A	K	Q	J	10	9	8	7
?	?	?	?	?	?	?	?
?	?	?	?	?	?	?	?
?	?	?	?	?	?	?	?
?	?	?	?	?	?	?	?

Game play: On the start signal, the first student on each team must run and take any card. If the card does not match the team's label, the player must lay the card back on the floor, face down, and go back to his/her team to tag the next player in line, who will then repeat this process. When a player finds a card that matches their team's label, he or she brings the card back to the team's location and places the card face up on the floor in front of their team. That student tags the next student in line, who then goes to take a card. This process continues until one team , locates their four cards.

Tips:

- Remind players that they must pay attention to their teammates' moves so they can avoid returning to cards that do not belong to their team.

85. PAPER SHOOT

Introduction: This is a game for two teams of 4 to 6 players per team. It's a good way to reinforce eye-hand coordination.

Equipment:

- batons made from rolled newspapers, about two-feet long

- paper wads or Nerf tennis balls

- one wastebasket

Game preparation: Divide the class into teams of four to six players. Designate a playing area and set the wastebasket in the middle of that area. Have one team surround the wastebasket, with players lying down on their backs, with their heads toward the wastebasket. The students' heads should be about a foot away from the basket. Give each of these players a baton. Mark off a restraining circle about ten feet away from the wastebasket. The second team must line up behind this circle.

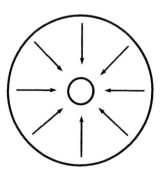

Game play: The outside team must try to shoot (underhand toss) the paper balls into the wastebasket. The team lying down has to defend the wastebasket with their batons. After a two-minute time period, count the number of paper balls in the garbage can, and have the teams switch places and repeat the process. The team with the most paper balls in the wastebasket is the winner.

Tip:

- Depending on the number of students in the class, you can either increase the number of players per team (to a maximum of eight) or divide the class into four teams of four to six players and have seveal games going at one time. The team with the overall highest number of baskets wins.

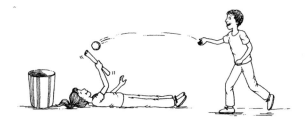

86. RUN AND RALLY

Grades 3–6

Introduction: This competitive game requires a lot of cooperation among players.

Equipment:

- 2 or 3 poly spots (one per team)

Game preparation: Divide the group into two or three teams of 8 to 10 players. Have each team line up behind a poly spot in file formation in the middle of the gym.

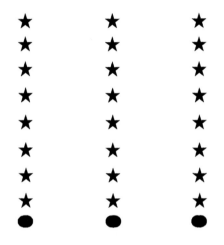

Game play: When you call out the command, "On the signal 'run' you need to touch something yellow… Ready? Run!" everyone on all of the teams must complete the assigned task and return to their starting line. (Obviously, not all students will complete the task in the same way, and that's fine.) When the students are starting to return to the starting line, call out "Rally!" and assign a line formation that the teams must make. (For example, you can tell the teams to line up by height, tallest to shortest.)

If playing with three teams, the first team to rally correctly earns three points, the second team two points and the third team one point. After doing this several times, the team with the most points wins.

Tips:

- Use your imagination for the first step in the command—for example, students may have to touch a specific wall, a mat, or any other object in the play area.

- To rally, try having team members line up by height; in alphabetical order by first name, last name, or middle name; or in birthday order.

- Try making the first step more challenging by having players touch two or more objects before returning to the starting line.

- Challenge the teams to see if they can play the game without talking.

- The game can be played with fewer people per team, but eight to ten players per team makes rallying more of a challenge.

87. ROB THE COOKIE JAR

Grades 3–6

Introduction: At one time or another, everyone has tried to get just one more cookie out of the cookie jar when no one was looking. Here's a fun team activity based on this concept.

Equipment:

- 16 beanbags
- 5 hoops

Game preparation: Arrange five hoops (cookie jars) as shown in the diagram. Place the beanbags (cookies) in the center cookie jar. Divide players into four teams and have each team form a line behind their own cookie jar.

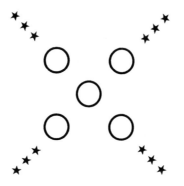

Game play: Each team's goal is to store a cache of six cookies. When you give the start signal, the first person on each team runs to the cookie jar to steal a cookie. After going to the cookie jar players place the cookie in their cookie jar and go to the back of their team's line. Players run to the cookie jar in the order in which they are in line. Players keep taking cookies from the middle jar until it is empty, at which point players can steal cookies from each other's cookie jars. Because no team can defend the cookies in its jar, there is always a place from which to steal a cookie. The first team to store up six cookies is the winner. A player may only take one cookie per turn

Tips:

- Teach players that strategy is important to winning in this game, because not only should they be working to get six cookies, but they should also try to take the cookies away from the teams closest to winning.

- If the game gets too easy, reduce the number of cookies available in the game or increase the number of cookies that a team must get to win.

- Make sure that only one player from a team is stealing at one time. It is easy for the players to get excited and begin stealing cookies out of turn.

88. GIVE AWAY

Introduction: Unlike Rob the Cookie Jar (see page 103), in this game players must give away objects instead of collect them.

Equipment:

- 24 beanbags
- 4 hoops

Game preparation: Arrange the hoops to form four corners of a square. (See the diagram for Rob the Cookie Jar on page 103, but leave out the center hoop.) Divide players into four teams and have each team form a line behind their own hoop. Place six beanbags in each hoop.

Game play: In this game, each team's goal is to give away all their beanbags. When you give the start signal, the first player on each team must run and give away one of the beanbags to any other team, return to his or her own team and tag the next player, then go to the back of the line. This process continues until one team has given away all of their beanbags and has an empty hoop.

Tip:

- If it's too difficult for players to give away all their beanbags, they may lose interest in the game. If you see this start to happen, stop the game and go on to another activity.

89. CLEAN UP THE TRASH

Grades 4–6

Introduction: This is a more advanced version of Rob the Cookie Jar (see page 103).

Equipment:

- 6 hoops
- 2 Koosh balls
- 2 deck tennis rings
- 24 beanbags
- 4 Whiffle balls (or substitute items)

Game preparation: Arrange the hoops as shown in the diagram. Divide the players into five or six equal teams and have each team form a line behind one of the outer hoops. In the center hoop, place two Koosh balls and two deck tennis rings. In each of the other hoops, place four beanbags and one Whiffle ball to represent the trash.

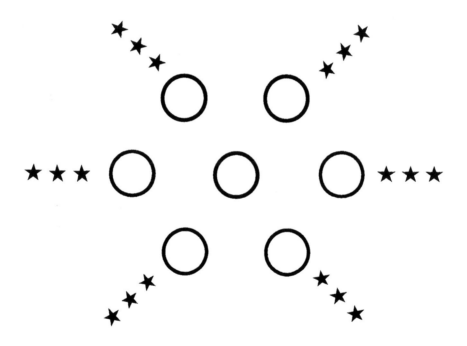

Game play: On the start signal, the first player in each line must grab the Whiffle ball, run to any hoop and give away the Whiffle ball and pick up one piece of trash to bring back to his or her team's hoop. That player then tags the next student in line, who must repeat the process, always taking any Whiffle ball that may have been deposited in the team's hoop. The person running may only carry one piece of trash at a time. An individual can also switch a piece of trash and bring back a different piece. Teams get one point for each Koosh ball, two points for each deck tennis ring and lose one point for each Whiffle ball in their hoop. At the end of the designated time period, the team with the most points wins.

90. SHIPWRECK

Introduction: This is a very fast moving game that requires the students to listen and follow directions. The game requires some knowledge of marine jargon, which adds to the fun.

Equipment: None

Game preparation: Mark your playing space as shown in the diagram. It is helpful to place signs on the walls to designate the four areas of a ship. Line up the players on the line in the stern. You will be the Captain and should stand in the middle of the playing area and give the orders.

Game play: As the Captain, you give out orders that the players (the crew) must carry out. Start out with orders that reinforce students' knowledge of the different parts of the ship. For example, give the command "To the bow." In response to this, the crew must run to and line up on the line representing the bow. When the crew knows where all four areas of the ship are located and they are moving without colliding with others, add other tasks that they need to remember and to perform. If the command doesn't call for them to go to another part of the ship, they are to perform the task in place.

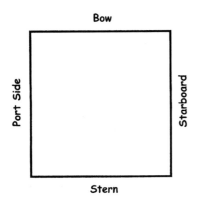

The last person to carry out a command receives a demerit. After acumulating three demerits for poor service, a player is sent to the brig (ship's jail). When an individual carries out a task and is definitely last, that person receives a demerit. To get out of the brig, a player should perform a quick, mildly unpleasant task.

Orders you, the Captain, can give the crew include:

- **Go to the stern (or the bow, starboard, or port side).** All players must run and line up on the designated area. This command can be combined with any of the following.

- **Hit the deck.** Players must lie down on their stomachs.

- **Swab the deck.** Players must pretend they are mopping the deck.

- **Person overboard.** Players pair up. One person gets on all fours (this is the ship's railing). The other player places one foot on the player's back and puts his/her hand over their brow to shade the sunshine from his/her eyes, so they can see someone in the sea.

- **Mates in the galley.** Players must make a group of three people and sit down holding hands.

- **Bring in the anchor.** Players pretend to be pulling in a heavy anchor.

- **Sharks!** Players lay down on their backs and stick one leg up in the air.

- **Man the Pumps.** This means the ship is taking on water. To remove the water everyone must get into push-up position and do push-ups, operating the pumps.

- **Seasick.** Players must grab their stomachs and moan.

Tip:

- Encourage the students to suggest their own tasks.

91. HAPPY HEALTH HABITS

Introduction: The game is played like Shipwreck (see page 106); however, it reinforces how exercise, diet, rest, and personal hygiene are an important part of a healthy lifestyle.

Equipment: None

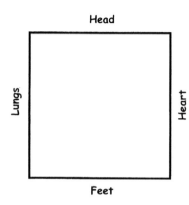

Game preparation: Label the four sides of the playing area to represent the head, heart, lungs, and feet. Have all players line up along one side of the area. Designate an area to represent the infirmary.

Game play: As the health specialist, you will give health-habit commands to the players. Start out by giving the players commands to go to the different body parts you've designated along the four sides of the gym. In response to your command, students must line up along the proper line.

When the players master this and can run to the proper line without colliding with others, add other tasks they need to remember and to perform—for example, command students to walk for fitness, in response to which students must walk in general space or to an area you specify. If your command doesn't call for them to go to another part of the playing area, they are to perform the task in place.

The student who cannot carry out a command receives a demerit. When an individual carries out a task and is definitely last, that person receives a demerit. After accumulating three demerits, a player is sent to the infirmary. To get out, a player should perform a quick, mildly unpleasant task.

Commands you can give students, either in combination with the command to go to another side of the play area or alone, include:

- **Pumping Iron.** Students pretend to be lifting weights.

- **Aerobic Dance.** Students do aerobic dance moves (or follow your aerobic moves).

- **Three Cheers for Exercise.** Shake hands with as many people as possible. One student says "Hip, hip." The other student responds loudly with "fitness."

- **Balance Your Diet.** Students make a four-person balance. While balancing, they each say one of the four food groups: protein, fruits and vegetables, dairy products, and carbohydrates.

- **Brush Your Teeth.** Students pretend to brush their teeth.

- **Bathe Regularly.** Students pretend to sing in the shower.

- **Good Posture.** Students walk with really good posture.

Tips:

- Be creative in thinking up commands.

- Allow students to suggest commands you can give

92. TRAVEL

Introduction: This game is similar in nature to Shipwreck except that the terminology used refers to various parts of North America.

Equipment: None

Game preparation: Label the four sides of the playing area with names of places in a particular region of the world. (North America is used In the diagram.) Have all players line up along one side.

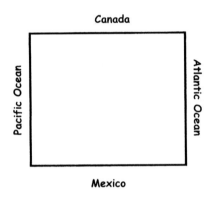

Game play: Begin the game by calling out destinations that the players must travel to. As students get the hang of getting from side to side without colliding with one another, have them travel by different means. For example, you might call out "Go to Canada by plane," to which students must respond by running to the Canada line with their arms outstretched. The student who does not get to the destination by the mode of travel you specify gets a summons. After accumulating three summonses a player pays a fine by going to a designated spot in the gym and performing a quick, mildly unpleasant task, after which the player can return to the game.

Travel plans you can call out include:

- **Take a car to_____.** All students must walk to the area designated and line up. They should pretend to hold a steering wheel as they move.

- **Go by train to_____.** Players get into groups of three or four and place their hands on the person's hips in front of them and move like a train to the area called.

- **Go by plane to_____.** Students pretend they are flying and run to the area called.

- **Climb a mountain.** Players get into groups of three and make a three-person pyramid. (Teach this before using it.)

- **Chop down a tree in the Northwest.** Players pretend they are chopping down a tree. When it falls, they yell "Timber."

- **Take a siesta in Mexico.** Everyone sits with their knees drawn up and their heads on their knees.

- **Take a subway in New York.** Players pair up, then one person straddles their legs, and the other person goes trough the tunnel. They continue by reversing this process until a new command is given.

- **Sunbathe in Mexico.** Players lounge in the sun.

- **Play Ball in_____.** Players pretend to swing a baseball bat.

Tip:

- Encourage the students to create their own tasks.

93. CHRISTMAS LAND

Grades K–4

Introduction: This game is similar to shipwreck and is a great activity to use during the Christmas Season.

Equipment: None

Game preparation: Mark your playing area as shown in the diagram. Start the game with all of the players lining up at the North Pole. Santa (the teacher) should stand in the center of the playing area.

Game play: Follow the instructions for shipwreck (see page 106), but use Christmas theme tasks. Here again, players who get three demerits for failing to finish an assigned task must perform a brief, slightly unpleasant but funny task to get back in the game. Commands you can use in this game include:

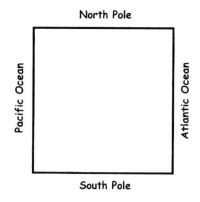

- Moving to the four basic areas of Christmas Land.

- **Hitch up the reindeer.** Students get into groups of three with two people in front facing forward inside hands joined, representing the reindeer, and the back person holding their outside hands and representing the driver of the sleigh. The sleigh doesn't travel; it just stays in place.

- **Clean up the workshop.** Players pretend that they are sweeping the floor.

- **Elf inspection.** This can only take place at the North Pole so no matter where the players are at when this command is given, they must go to the North Pole. Once they are there, everyone lines up and salutes Santa showing they are ready for inspection.

- **Gather around the Christmas tree.** Players get into groups of three and hold hands skipping in a small circle.

- **Trains around the Christmas tree.** Players grab onto another person's hips and using a shuffle step move around making sounds like a train. The lines can be two or more people long.

- **Seasons Greetings.** Players shake hands with as many people as possible. If one person says Merry Christmas the other must respond with Happy New Year or vice versa.

- **Imitate various toys.** Some traditional toys would be Robots (children move around stiffly); Jack-in-the-box (children jump up and down and say Merry Christmas at the top of every jump); and Music Box (children turn around as a ballet dancer would on top of a music box). Make up movements for the hottest toys which the children are interested.

- There are countless commands you can give with this game.

Tip:

- Be creative.

94. FISH GOBBLER

Introduction: This cooperative activity can inspire interest in marine life.

Equipment: None

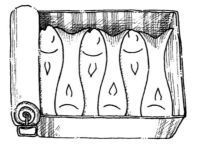

Game preparation: All of the students line up on one end line in the playing area. The Fish Gobbler (preferably the teacher) takes a place in the center of the playing area.

Game play: When the Fish Gobbler gives the command "Ship," all of the players must run toward the opposite wall. On the command "Shore," everyone must run back toward the starting line. The Fish Gobbler continues to call out these two commands and move the players back and forth. In addition, at any time the Fish Gobbler can also give one of the following signals:

- **Fishnet.** Students drop to the floor on their stomachs and begin joining hands, feet, legs, etc. so that all of the students are linked together as a fish net. The goal for the students is to complete the task in five seconds.

- **Rescue.** When a task has been completed, the Fish Gobbler calls "rescue" and all of the students get up and get prepared to respond to the next command, usually either Ship or Shore.

- **Sardines.** Everyone runs to a central point and begins to make the tightest group possible by forming a massive standing hug.

- **Iceberg.** All players freeze.

- **Crabs:** Everyone needs to be able to hold hands with two other people by bending over and reaching their hands through their legs.

- **Fishermen:** Everyone finds a partner. One person kneels on one knee and places the other leg so their partner can sit on their knee. The person sitting on the knee pretends to hold a fish pole.

Tips:

- The game can be played on a cooperative basis by challenging students to have everyone accomplish the tasks in five seconds.

- To make the game more interesting, the Fish Gobbler can catch students who cannot get into the formation quickly enough to be safe.

95. BILLY GOATS AND COWS

Grades 3–6

Introduction: This is a quiet game that does not require physical skill. It's included because it teaches the value of cooperation and is an excellent cool down, icebreaker, or classroom activity. A good way to introduce the game is to talk about the sounds that the farm animals make.

Equipment: Blindfolds, if possible, for all players

Game preparation: Divide the class into two equal groups: the Billy Goats and the Cows. In a scatter formation, mix everybody together in a small area—a space approximately 20′ × 20′ is appropriate.

Game play: Before starting the activity, have all the students close their eyes and turn around three times as fast as they can. Keeping their eyes closed, players set out to find a member of their team. The only words that the Billy Goats can say are "Baa baa, " and the only words the Cows may say are "Moo moo." When two people touch, they shake hands and make their sounds. If both turn out to be from the same team, they join hands and continue playing while holding hands. The goal is for all the members of a team to end up in one long chain. If in walking around and meeting other players two players from opposite teams greet each other with their animal sounds, they simply leave each other and continue searching for their own teammates. It is important to emphasize that the only time players can make their sound is when they are shaking hands.

Tips:

- Make sure no one wanders too far from the playing area.

- When you no longer hear one of the sounds, stop the game and check to see if one team is all in a line.

96. SHERLOCK HOLMES: The Case of Mr. Freeze

Grades 4–6

Introduction: In this game, everyone is a detective trying to identify the guilty party. Set the stage for the game by telling a story about people who have a special chemical they use to temporarily freeze people. These culprits are wanted by the law and Sherlock Holmes is out to apprehend them.

Equipment: None

Game preparation: Have all of the participants scatter and sit down in an area about 30' square. Secretly, select two to four people to be Mr. or Ms. Freeze. (There should be one Mr. or Ms. Freeze for every ten to twelve players.)

Game play: As the game starts, players move slowly around the area and make eye contact with each person they meet. The eye contact should be exaggerated to assure that everyone does make eye contact. The "freezers" make eye contact just like everyone else, except they may also wink at someone while making eye contact with them. A freezer has to be discreet and does not have to wink at everyone with whom he or she makes eye contact.

A person who has been winked at is frozen and should wait until the freezer is two or more steps away (so as not to give away the secret of who the freezer is) and then very dramatically crumple to the floor and remain frozen. This act should draw all the other players' attention. As the game progresses and a player thinks they can identify Mr. or Ms. Freeze, a player announces. "I have an accusation." If another player says I second the accusation, the teacher stops the game and counts "1,2,3" and on "3" both players must point at the person they are accusing. If both accusers point at the same person, and that player is a freezer, the freezer is removed from the game. However, if the accusers pick a player who is not a freezer or if they do not pick the same person, the accusers freeze and crumple to the floor on the spot and the freezer remains unidentified.

The game continues until all of the freezers have been found or until the freezers have frozen everyone.

112

97. STONE FACE

Grades 3–6

Introduction: Stone Face allows players to improve their concentration and control of their emotions.

Equipment: None

Game preparation: Divide players into two equal teams and have the teams line up about six feet apart, with players from the same team being about arms length apart.

Game play: The first player on each team steps out into the space between the teams. They stand at opposite ends of the formation facing each other. These players turn their faces into stony glares and stare into the eyes of their opponent. As both players walk slowly toward each other, members of the opposite team try to make the challenger from the opposite team break into a smile or a laugh. If they succeed, the opponent must join their team. The game continues until there is only one person remaining on one team or each player has had a turn. The winning team will be the largest team at the end of the game.

98. GREAT BANK ROBBERY

Grades 4–6

Introduction: This is a take off on the traditional game Capture the Flag. To be successful, a team will have to use teamwork and strategy.

Equipment:

- identification vests for each team
- 4 balls or bowling pins

Game preparation: Divide players into two teams and assign each team to one-half of the playing area. Have players of each team wear vests of the same color. Set up the playing area as shown in the diagram. Place two large balls or bowling pins in each team's bank to represent the gold. Each team must select a jail keeper, who will stand by the jail, and a guard to stand near the bank. The remaining students scatter on their half of the floor.

Game play: Players must try to steal the gold from the other team's bank; however players may only grab one gold nugget at a time. When they venture into the enemy's territory, players may be tagged and jailed by an opponent. If tagged they go to that team's jail. The guard may run across the bank when chasing someone but may never guard the gold by standing inside the bank.

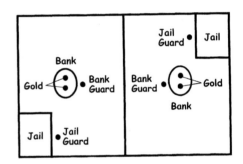

Players can escape from jail if a teammate can reach and tag them without being caught; however, if either player is tagged on the way back to their own side both players will go to jail. Players can also escape from jail by grabbing the jail keeper and pulling him or her into jail. If this is accomplished, a jailbreak is declared and all prisoners are free to try and reach safety. Prisoners may not step out of the jail area to grab the jail guard. A player fleeing from jail may not steal the gold on the way to safety.

If a student who has picked up the gold and is trying to reach safety is caught, the gold is returned to the bank and that student goes to jail. The gold may not be passed from player to player.

The game continues until one side has confiscated all of the other team's gold or until all the players from one side are jailed.

Tips:

- Teach students how to strategize their attacks. For example, you can suggest that a team send in two or three students to free prisoners and two other players from different directions to steal the gold.
- A large area—at least 40' × 60'—is needed for this game. Playing in a larger area outdoors is even better.

114

99. GOLD RUNNER

Introduction: This game is similar to Great Bank Robbery (see page 114), but includes some new twists.

Equipment:

- identification vests for each team
- 4 balls or bowling pins
- 4 or more poly spots or hoops

Game preparation: Set the play area up the same as for Great Bank Robbery, but eliminate the jails and place two or three poly spots or hoops within each team's territory to serve as safe areas where an intruder cannot be caught.

Game play: The rules are the same as for Great Bank Robbery, but with the following changes: Instead of going to jail, a player who is caught on enemy turf is frozen and must stand in one place in a hands-up position. A frozen student can be rescued if two teammates can take the frozen student by the hands and run him or her back to safety; however, if one of the three is tagged, the whole group must freeze in enemy territory.

If a trespasser is caught with a piece of gold, the gold is reclaimed by the opposing side and instead of being frozen, the player changes sides. This will allow each team the opportunity to increase in size.

The game continues until one side has confiscated all of the other team's gold or until all the players from one side are frozen or have switched sides.

115

Section 7

SMALL GROUP GAMES

Small group games are just what the name implies, activities for two to five children. To use these games in physical education class, you simply group children into several small groups of the correct size. Small group games allow for natural leadership to emerge and provide maximum participation for all players. Because there are only a few children playing in the group, each must do his or her part or the game will not be successful.

After playing a small group game, ask the children to make up a variation of the game they played or create a small group game of their own. Sometimes they will surprise you.

100. PUSH-UP DUEL

Introduction: This is a good activity to work out the upper body in a way other than doing push-ups. The activity keeps the upper body weight on the arms and shoulders so those areas are used vigorously. You can use this as a fitness station or partner activity. The students enjoy it and forget they are working on fitness.

Equipment: None

Game preparation: Group the children in pairs. Partners must assume a push-up position facing each other with their heads six inches apart.

Game play: When you give the start signal, each partner must try to tag the other's hands as many times as possible in a designated time limit. (Thirty seconds to one minute is an ideal amount of time.) Although the main objective is to score points by touching a partner's hands, tell players that it is just as important to try and avoid being tagged.

Tip:

- When in the push-up position, students have a natural tendency to spread their legs apart for more stability. Encourage them to keep their legs and feet together.

101. PUSH-UP TIC TAC TOE

Introduction: This partner activity is a novel method of playing Tic Tac Toe and is a good way to get children to enjoy doing push-ups.

Equipment:

- 1 Tic Tac Toe board per set of partners
- 8 beanbags (4 each of two different colors) per set of partners

Game preparation: Group children in pairs. Partners must get into push-up position, one on each side of the Tic Tac Toe board. They must play a game of Tic Tac Toe, remaining in push-up position until the game is ended. Have the players decide who will go first. Have as many games going as possible to minimize waiting time.

Game play: On the start signal both players do a push-up together. After the push-ups the first player places a beanbag on the board. They both do a second push-up and the second player places a beanbag on the board. Play continues in this fashion until there is a winner or the game is a scratch.

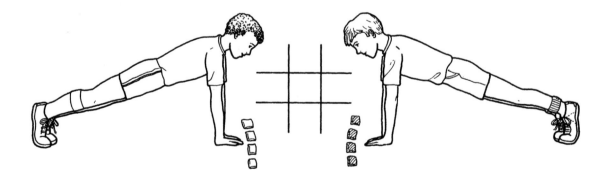

102. TOE TAG

Introduction: This is a high-energy activity that can serve as a general partner activity as well as a fitness station.

Equipment:

- 1 beanbag per student

Game preparation: Pair up all the students and give each a beanbag.

Game play: When you give the start signal, each student must try to "tag" his or her partner by throwing the beanbag at the partner's toes. Students have to keep track of how many times they "tag" their partners toes in one minute.

After each toss of the beanbag, students need to retrieve their original beanbag. After one minute, everyone should get a new partner and repeat the activity.

Tip:

- Remind players that they are expected to stay in the small area where they begin and not to run around the entire floor space.

103. CIRCLE TAG

Grades 2–6

Introduction: Circle tag is a fast moving game that emphasizes lateral movement.

Equipment: None

Game preparation: Organize children into groups of 4. Three players must hold hands to form a circle; the fourth player is "it" and must stand outside the circle. (See the diagram.)

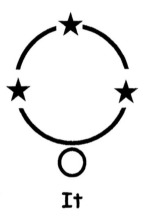

It

Game play: The "it" must catch the player standing directly opposite him or her in the circle. The players in the circle have to work together moving laterally in the circle—sliding to the right or to the left—to prevent that person from being caught. The "it" may not reach over or under the circle to tag the player. When "it" tags the player, the two change roles. The new "it" must chase a person who has not been chased yet or who hasn't been chased for a while.

Tip:

- Give children time to practice sliding in a circle both to the left and to the right before playing the game.

104. CYCLONE RELAY

Introduction: Just as a cyclone moves in a circular pattern, the runners in this race will also move in a fast circular pattern.

Equipment: None

Game preparation: Organize teams of 5 or 6 players. Each team starts in a circle with all players laying on their backs, heads to the middle of the circle. Players number off in consecutive order.

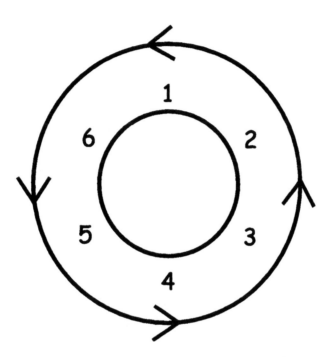

Game play: On the start signal, player 1 starts by running around the circle moving toward player 2. After going around the circle once, player 2 follows 1. As they come around the circle the next time, player 3 follows. This continues until all of the players are up and running. When the entire team is in line and running, player 1 stops at his or her starting position and lays down. On the next lap around player 2 stops and lays down. Subsequently, as each player's turn comes, they lay down in their starting positions until the last player is down. The first team to be back in starting formation is the winner.

Tip:

- In a gymnasium with several groups moving at once, the circles cannot be too large; however, when played outdoors, students can be placed in a circle about 25 feet in diameter, giving the opportunity to get a strenuous workout.

105.   HUMAN HURDLE

Introduction: This game combines some of the elements of Cyclone Relay (see page 123) with the thrill of leaping over a live body.

Equipment: None

Game preparation: Group children into teams of 5 or 6 players. All players must lay on their stomachs with their head to the middle of the circle. The players number off in consecutive order.

Game play: On the start signal, player 1 starts running around the circle moving toward player 2, and leaping over each person along the way. Players should leap over the people by crossing their bodies between the waist and the knees. When player 1 returns to their original position, player 2 takes off and does the same thing. When all players have had a turn and every member of the team is back in the starting position, the team is finished. The team whose members get all the way around and back into starting formation first is the winner.

106. FOUR-IN-A-LINE

Introduction: Here is a great way to teach children the importance of team work.

Equipment: None

Game preparation: Designate two goal lines on opposite sides of the playing area. Players must line up in the middle of the playing area in groups of four, with all of the players facing the same direction and holding hands.

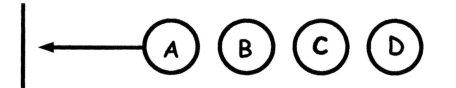

Game play: On the start signal each team runs toward Line one. The only player on the team who can touch that line is the player closest to line one (player A in the diagram). When the team touches the line, player "A" yells "1" (meaning it is the first time he or she has touched the line 1). At that moment, the entire team starts running toward the opposite line. The only player who can touch this line is player D. When player "D" touches line II, player "D" yells "1" (meaning it is the first time he or she has touched line II). Now the team moves back across the playing area to touch the first goal line. Player "A" now yells "2" when he or she touches the line. The team again moves toward the opposite line, which player "D" must touch. Upon touching the line "D" yells "2." This procedure is repeated one more time. When both player "A" and "D" have made the third touches on their respective lines, the team heads back to the middle of the playing area where they started and stops there. The first team to make it back to the starting position is the winner.

107. CHARIOT RACE

Introduction: This activity offers a good opportunity to teach players the value of cooperation and have them practice running.

Equipment: None

Game preparation: Designate a starting line and a goal line facing each other about 40 feet apart. Divide the class into teams of three and have the teams line up behind the starting line. Two players on each team must join inside hands and stand on the starting line. (These players represent the chariot.) The third player must stand behind the first two and hold the outside hand of each player. (This person is the driver.)

Game play: When you give the start signal, the driver of each team must move the chariot to the goal line and back. Upon reaching the starting line, the driver switches with one of the horses and the new driver drives the chariot to the goal line and back. When all the players have been the driver, that team is finished. The first team to finish is the winner.

108. LIMOUSINE SERVICE

Introduction: The rules for this game are exactly the same as for the Chariot Race (see page 126) except for the method of transportation.

Equipment: None

Game preparation: Designate a starting line and a goal line facing each other and about 40 feet apart. Divide the class into teams of three and have the teams line up behind the starting line. Two players on each team stand facing each other, slightly behind the starting line. These players must join both hands straight across (forming the "limousine"). The third player stands on the starting line in front of the limousine.

Game play: When you give the start signal, the pair of players holding hands (the limousine) form a chair by lowering their front arms to chair level and moving their back arms into position to be the back of the chair. The third person sits down in the chair and the limousine picks him or her up and begins to move to the goal line and back. Once the team makes it back to the starting line, a new player gets carried to the goal line and back. After all of the team's members have ridden in the limousine, the team is finished. The first team to finish and get back to the starting line is the winner.

109. TRAIN RELAY

Grades 3–6

Introduction: This activity reinforces the importance of cooperation. It keeps everyone moving and actively involved.

Equipment:

- 2 cones per team to mark the figure–eight course

Game preparation: Designate a starting line. Divide the class into teams of four and have the teams line up in single file behind the starting line, each player holding on to the hips of the player in front. Place a cone in front of each team about 15 feet away from the starting line, and another about 30 feet away.

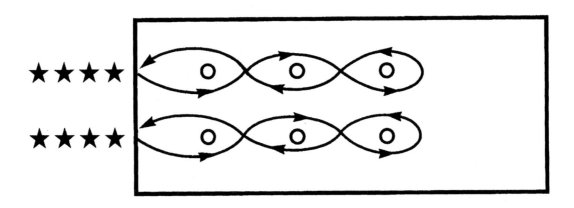

Game play: On the start signal, each team moves as a group around the cones and back to the starting line in a figure eight pattern. Upon completing the first trip through the course, the lead person goes to the rear of the train and the new leader takes the team through the course again. Upon ending the second trip through the course, the leader goes to the rear of the train and the procedure is repeated again until everyone has been the leader. When the team gets back from the last trip and into their starting position, the team is finished. The first team to finish is the winner.

110. FOLLOW THE LEADER

Grades 3–6

Introduction: This small group activity works great as a warm-up activity and is a good task for fostering cooperation and group spirit. It also gives everyone in the group an opportunity to be a responsible leader.

Equipment:

- CD player
- music CDs

Game preparation: Organize the class into groups of 5 or 6, and have the groups stand in single file lines scattered throughout the general area. Whoever is in the front of each line is the leader.

Game play: When you start the music and call out a category of movement—such as locomotion, exercise, or dance—the leader of each team must lead the group in the designated style of movement. Team leaders can be creative in the movement they choose, as long as it fits one of the categories you designate:

Locomotion—the leader leads the group single file through general space using a walk, run, jump, hop, leap, gallop, slide, skip or a combination of those movements.

Exercise—the leader leads the groups in a calisthenic movement

Dance—the leader leads the group in an aerobic dance type of movement or a dance pattern.

Each turn should last about 30 seconds to a minute. When you stop the music the turn ends, the leaders go to the back of their line and the next person in line for each team becomes the new leader.

Tip:

- This activity can be simplified for younger students by using just one category of movement.

111. PONY EXPRESS RUN

Grades 3–6

Introduction: Pony Express Run is a relay game. It is a very good cardiovascular exercise. It's best to play this game outdoors.

Equipment:

- 1 track baton for each team

Game preparation: Mark a track similar to the one shown in the diagram. Designate four stations on the track, but don't make the stations too far apart—a distance of 50 yards between stations is recommended. Group students into teams of four. Assign a member of each team to each station. All teams go at the same time on the same track.

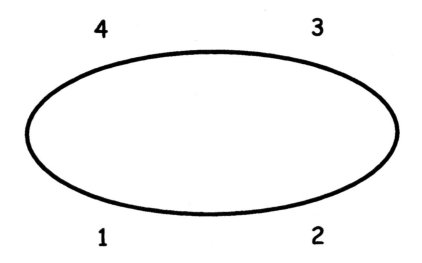

Game play: Player 1 starts the race by carrying the baton to player 2. Player 1 stays at station 2. Player 2 carries the baton to player 3 and stays at station 3. Player 3 carries the baton to player 4 and stays at station 4. Player 4 has to carry the baton all the way to player 1, who is at station 2. This is double duty for player 4. Player 4 stays at station 2.

This continues until all of the runners are back in their starting positions. The runner that has to run the longer stretch will change on every circuit. The team finishing first is the winner or each team could be timed and they could try a second time to improve their score.

Tips:

- Although this may sound complicated, it usually works out smoothly.
- If the students have been taught how to pass a baton for a pursuit relay, this game gives them an excellent opportunity to practice the hand-offs.

Section 8

COOPERATIVE GAMES AND ACTIVITIES

When children are taught the fundamentals of cooperation, they learn to understand more about communication, cohesiveness, and trust. They also develop positive social interaction skills.

Cooperative games and activities emphasize a spirit of acceptance, teamwork, and sharing. For this chapter, a cooperative activity will be defined as one that is noncompetitive and encourages interaction between people. It is important that everyone feels involved and partially responsible for the outcome of the game.

To foster teamwork, it helps to discuss some of these concepts with the participants before beginning an activity:

Using the following concepts may help develop a discussion to make the key concepts of cooperation make sense to younger students:

1. Who is your favorite person to spend time with?

2. What made this person your favorite?

3. Who is your ideal playmate?

4. What makes an enjoyable playing experience?

You might also ask the group to name several phrases or words that describe cooperation. After they have offered some ideas, have the group go back and define the phrases. Challenge them to apply those concepts in the upcoming activities.

In a cooperative activity every student should experience:

1. **Equality:** An equal opportunity for input and participation.

2. **Participation** An opportunity to be successful.

3. **Trust:** Trust in his or her teammates.

If these 4 components can be implemented in the activity, the goal becomes to complete the task or to improve the group's performance.

In a cooperative activity, no player should be hailed as the star or singled out as the worst player. The spirit of cooperation should become more important than the game.

This section includes partner, small group, and large group activities. There is no set progression for cooperative activities, so the activities are listed in alphabetical order. A suggested ability level is included to indicate at what grade levels the activity might be most appropriate.

112. BACK–TO–BACK GET UP

Grades K–6

Introduction: Start this challenge as a partner activity. Continue combining smaller groups until you have one large (class) group trying the challenge together.

Equipment: None

Game preparation: Have partners stand back to back.

Game play: Partners should hook elbows together and sit down cooperatively by pressing their backs together. From the sitting position, they should move their feet close to their bottoms and stand back up as a unit.

Tips:

- Try it without hooking elbows—no hands!

113.   BARNYARD

Introduction: The objective of this large group activity is to create a team of "animals." It is not a race.

Equipment: Blindfolds

Game preparation: Blindfold the players and scatter them in the play space.

Game play: Walk among the players and whisper one of three or four farm animal names to each person such as cow, horse, chicken, and pig.

On the signal "go," the players should begin to move around searching for people who have the same animal name. When they meet someone, they should shake hands and make the sound of their animal. For instance, pigs go "oink, oink," cows go "moo, moo," horses go, "nay, nay," and chickens go, "cluck, cluck." They may only speak if they are shaking hands. As the players find members of their group, they should join hands and go searching for more teammates.

The objective is to find all of your animals not to see who can do it fastest.

114. BATTLESHIP

Introduction: Kids love this safe form of dodgeball. It is quite different from normal dodgeball games and requires cooperation from the team.

Equipment:

- a sturdy blanket or tumbling mat for each team
- 3 nerf balls for each team

Game preparation: Group the players into teams of 7. Line up 6 people along the edges of the battleship (mat or blanket). The seventh player is the Captain, who sits on the mat with three spongy cannonballs.

Game play: The Captain of the ship should direct the crew to pull the ship (mat or blanket) to the most strategic position from which to fire on another ship. To score a hit, and to earn 5 points, a ball must hit the Captain of another ship. The hit must be direct; it cannot rebound off the mat and then hit the Captain. Crew members may try to deflect balls that threaten to hit the Captain.

Whenever a ship has been hit, a new team member is selected to be the Captain. The team scoring the hit cannot fire on that ship twice in a row.

After running out of cannonballs, the Captain directs the crew to pull the battleship over to balls that have already been fired. The crew may pick the balls up off the floor and give them to the Captain, but they may never leave the ship.

Tip:

- Rubber balls should never be used in this safe game.

115. BLIND BALL RETRIEVAL

Grades 4–6

Introduction: Blind Ball Retrieval requires concentration and is useful for developing trust between players.

Equipment:

- several soft balls

Game preparation: Divide the players into groups of 6 or 8 players and have the groups gather around the center of the play area.

Game play: Each group blindfolds half of its players. On "go," toss several foam balls into the center of the play area. Each team's sighted players must direct the blindfolded players, without touching them, to retrieve as many balls as possible. Each ball that is retrieved counts as one point.

Tips:

- Because you will have three or four different teams shouting directions at the same time, the blindfolded retrievers may have trouble understanding what to do. This can be frustrating but also makes the game more interesting. You might suggest to the teams that they work out a strategy to help the blindfolded players discern which directions are for them.

116. BLINDFOLDED FOOTBALL

Grades 2–6

Introduction: Blindfolded teammates must coordinate their actions to accumulate points. This is a good station activity, it might be helpful to introduce the concept of giving directions to blindfolded players by participating in the Blizzard activity first.

Equipment:

- 1 nerf football per group
- chalk or string for goal line

Game preparation: Divide the players into groups of four (a coach, a center, a holder, and a kicker) and line up each team about 20 feet from the goal line. All the players are blindfolded except for the coach.

Game play: The center hikes ball to the holder and the kicker tries to kick the ball across the goal line. If a center hike to the holder goes astray, the coach needs to direct the holder to the ball so that the play can continue. One point is scored for a successful kick. After each kick the team members rotate to a new position. After all the positions have been played, the team totals its score.

117. BLIZZARD

Introduction: This partner activity is a good introduction to Blindfold Football or any other activity that requires giving instructions to blindfolded teammates. Set the stage for this activity by discussing how difficult it is to see anything during a blizzard.

Equipment:

- blindfolds
- a simple obstacle course consisting of several challenges to go over, under, in, and between

Game preparation: Assign one or 2 sets of partners per station, one partner should be blindfolded

Game play: The sighted partner should guide the blindfolded partner through the obstacle course using only verbal commands. Partners are never allowed to touch each other unless necessary for safety reasons.

Tip:

- The person giving the directions should be encouraged to use complete sentences for each direction.

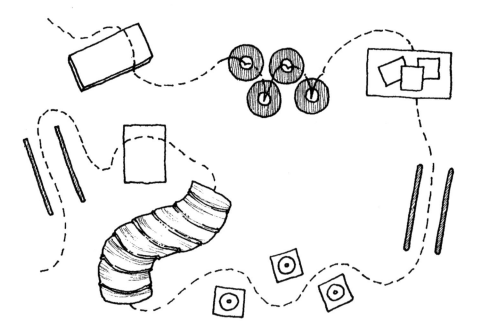

118. BODY JUMPING

Introduction: This body jumping activity can go on all day! Before you begin, have a discussion on safe jumping procedures. Demonstrate this with several capable students.

Equipment: None

Game preparation: Line up players about two feet apart and on their stomachs. Their heads should face in the same direction.

Game play: The player at the back of the line stands up and begins to leap over every player in the line. As soon as the first player has leaped over the second player, the second player should jump up and begin leaping down the line. When each player reaches the head of the line he or she should lie down. Passing is not allowed. When students finish the line and get ready to lay down it is okay to curve the line.

119. BOOP

Introduction: The challenge is to keep the balloon afloat (off the floor) by batting the balloon only with the part of the body specified. This could also be a station activity.

Equipment:

• 2 or 3 large balloons per group

Game preparation: Divide the class into groups of 6 or 8 players and have each group join hands in a circle. They must keep their hands joined at all times.

Game play: Instruct the groups to keep 1 balloon afloat using only their hands. Have them count to determine their team's best effort. Next, try using only elbows, heads, knees, feet, or blowing.

When it is to easy for a group to keep one balloon afloat, add 2 or 3 balloons.

Tips:

• Have the players try the game again lying down on their backs with their heads almost touching at the center of a circle. They should continue to hold hands.

140

120. CATERPILLAR

Introduction: Players will learn how to coordinate their movements so that they can walk as a group in an awkward position.

Equipment:

• a simple obstacle course

Game preparation: Players line up standing one behind the other. Have them place their hands on the ankles of the person in front of them. Start with four to eight people per group.

Game play: Instruct the players to move forward as a group.

Tips:

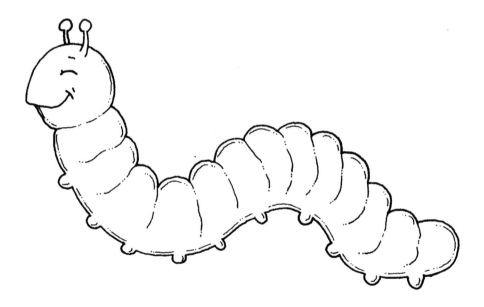

• After they have developed a system of cooperative movement, have them try to caterpillar-walk through the obstacle course. Later see if the caterpillar can make up a dance sequence.

121. CENTIPEDE

Grades K–4

Introduction: Begin this clever activity as a partner stunt and increase the group size as the ability level allows. Your players will imitate the multilegged centipede. It takes thinking and cooperation to get all of the legs to move at the right time!

Equipment: None

Game preparation: One player gets down on hands and feet and elevates his or her behind. The second player gets into the same position and crawls under and between the first player's legs.

Game play: The second player lifts up the first player, who places his or her feet on the second player's waist. The pair should now have four hands and two feet on the floor.

Tip:

- When the team can move successfully, add a third player.

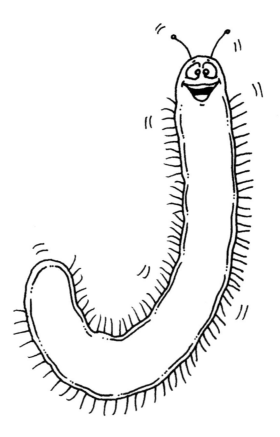

122. CINDERELLA'S SHOES

Introduction: This activity follows the Cinderella story. If you think the girl/boy issue will make anyone uncomfortable, call it the "magic shoe" instead.

Equipment:

- blindfolds for each Prince Charming

Game preparation: Arrange the class in a double circle, where every player is facing a partner. The inside circle will consist of blindfolded Prince Charmings. The outside circle will be full of Cinderellas.

Game play: Before being blindfolded each Prince Charming should remove Cinderella's shoes and place them in the middle of the circle.

After the leader mixes up the shoes each Cinderella gives oral directions to a blindfolded Prince Charming about how to find her shoes and to put them on her.

Tips:

- Since you will have several Cinderellas shouting directions at the same time, the princes may have trouble understanding what to do. This can be frustrating but also makes the game more interesting. You might suggest to the teams that they work out a strategy to help the blindfolded players discern which directions are for them.

123. COOPERATIVE MUSICAL CHAIRS

Introduction: A take off on the old musical chairs. But in this version, nobody is eliminated.

Equipment:

- 1 chair for every two players
- music

Game preparation: Arrange the chairs back-to-back in two rows and the players in a circle around them.

```
O   O   O   O   O   O   O   O   O   O

O     ★   ★   ★   ★   ★   ★   ★     O

O       ★   ★   ★   ★   ★   ★   ★   O

O   O   O   O   O   O   O   O   O   O
```

| O = students |
| ★ = chairs |

Game play: When the music starts, the players walk clockwise around the chairs. When the music stops, everyone sits down. Instead of eliminating the players who do not find a chair, have them sit on the other players' knees. When everyone has been seated, start the music, remove a chair or two and repeat. Continue playing until they can't hold everyone on the remaining chairs. It is possible to get the whole class on one chair!

124. COOPERATIVE WALK TAG

Grades 2–4

Introduction: If you want to entertain a large group of players, try this wild game of tag. There are actually several games going on at once. The team approach keeps it civilized.

Equipment: None

Game preparation: Find a partner and hook elbows. Two pairs of players are assigned to a team of four and one pair is "it." Elbows must stay locked at all times and everyone must walk quickly. All of the sets of partners are moving and following pathways at the same time.

Game play: "It" counts to ten while the other pair hides amidst other teams in the play area. When "it" finds and catches the other half of the team, the roles are reversed. This means that all of the couples are following a pathway in the play area. The couple being chased just wants to get as many other couples between them and their "its" as possible. Other games are going on at the same time. The movement of the other players allows the fleeing group to hide.

125. DRESS ME

Introduction: This is the team approach to getting dressed. Players should have an opportunity to try both roles in the game.

Equipment:

- 1 large shirt per group

Game preparation: Organize players into groups of four. In each group, one player puts on a very large shirt and joins hands with a partner.

Game play: The partners wearing the shirt must continue to hold hands while the two other players try to move the shirt from the first player to the second. The shirt will be turned inside out during this process.

126. ELECTRIC FENCE

Grades 2–6

Introduction: The challenge to this game is to move each team member through a hole in an "electric fence" without touching the sides of the hole.

Equipment:

- volleyball standards
- stretch rope
- crash mat

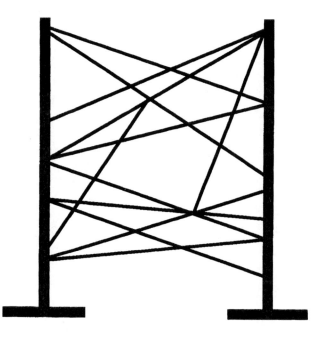

Game preparation: Stretch the rope back and forth between the standards so it looks like a spider web. Leave one hole large enough for a body to pass through. This web represents the electric fence. Place a crash mat under the electric fence. The hole should be about 30–36 inches off the floor. Create groups of five to seven students.

Game play: The entire team starts on one side of the electric fence. Teammates need to help each other through the hole without touching the electric fence. It is usually necessary for teammates to physically pick up a player and pass them through the hole. The hole is high enough that a player cannot step through it alone. No one is allowed to touch the fence. Once a team member has passed through to the other side, that player must stay there. No one is allowed to dive through the fence.

When a person touches the fence, that person must start over.

127.   FRANTIC

Introduction: The objective is for the whole class to keep a group of balls in motion at once. It is a good lead-up activity to soccer.

Equipment:

- 1 ball per every two participants

- stop watch

- boundary markers, such as cones

Game preparation: Scatter the players throughout the play area and give half of them a ball.

Game play: On the signal "go," start the stopwatch. Every player with a ball passes it on, soccer style. Any player can kick any ball in an attempt to keep all the balls in motion and in bounds. The group starts with five points, but a point is lost every time the instructor spots a ball that is not moving or a ball that has gone out of bounds. Click the stopwatch after five points. Keep track of how long the group kept the balls in motion. If the task is too easy, add a ball every 15 seconds.

128. FRANTIC BALLOON

Grades K–6

Introduction: This is the same game as Frantic, except that balloons are used instead of balls.

Equipment:

- 1 balloon per every two participants
- stop watch
- boundary markers, such as cones

Game preparation: Scatter the players throughout the play area and give half of them a balloon.

Game play: On the signal "go," start the stopwatch. Every player with a balloon taps it into the air, using any part of the body. No balloon can be caught at any time and nobody can hit the same balloon twice in a row. The group starts with five points, but a point is lost every time you spot a balloon that has touched the floor or a balloon that has gone out of bounds. Stop the stopwatch after five points are lost. Keep track of how long the group kept the balloons in motion. If the task is too easy, add a balloon every 15 seconds.

Tips:

- Students can also hold hands with a partner.

129. GIANT CRAB

Introduction: This activity will create a multilegged crab.

Equipment: None

Game preparation: 2 players stand one behind the other, facing in the same direction.

Game play: Ask the players to get into a crab walk position, that is, tell them to sit with their legs extended, feet on the floor, and their hands resting on the floor at either side of their hips. They should move into and between the legs of the person behind them. Then each player should place his or her arms over the legs of the player behind, while keeping their hands on the floor. There should be 8 body parts touching the floor. The Giant Crab should be able to move either forward or backward.

130. GIANT TURTLE

Introduction: Kids love this one! Before you begin, have a short discussion about a turtle's body and speed.

Equipment:

- a 5-foot x 10-foot tumbling mat for each group

Game preparation: Divide the players into groups of 6 and ask them to get on their hands and knees next to the mat.

Game play: Each group gets on their hands and knees. They balance the mat, which represents the turtle's shell, on the backs of each group. Ask the players to practice moving cooperatively, without dropping the mat (no hands allowed!).

Tips:

- You may enjoy having a turtle race. But instead of seeing who can go the fastest, see which team can go the farthest without losing its shell.

131. GROUP JUGGLE

Introduction: This is one of the ultimate group-throwing-and-catching games.

Equipment:

- 1 small ball for every person in the group

Game preparation: Arrange a group of about six players in a circle, about two steps apart from each other. Count off the players in a logical sequence, as shown in the diagram and put all of the balls on the floor behind player 1.

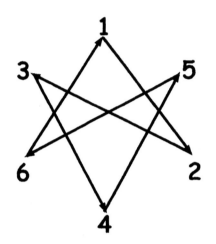

Game play: Player 1 starts the action by throwing to player 2. Player 2 throws to player 3, and so on. When the players have the pattern mastered, have player 1 start a second ball immediately after tossing the first ball. Keep adding balls seeing how many balls a team can keep in play.

Tip:

- Try to add a ball for every player in the circle.

132. HOG CALL

Introduction: Players rely on a special phrase to reunite with a partner.

Equipment:

- blindfolds for players

Game preparation: Pair off players and ask each team to decide on two words that go together, such as 'salt and pepper.' Then move them to opposite sides of the play area and blindfold them (or tell them to keep their eyes closed).

Game play: On the signal "go" the players call out half of their special phrase ("Salt, salt.") while walking carefully around the play area. They stop when they locate their partner.

Tip:

- An alternative method would be to specify that players can only say their word when they meet another player and shake hands with them. They do this until they find their partners.

133. HOOP PASS

Introduction: This activity can be done with one hoop by itself or with several hoops going at once. These directions apply to using multiple hoops. This is a popular Play Day activity.

Equipment:

- 15 hoops per group

Game preparation: Line up players and ask them to hold hands. Place the pile of hoops close to the first player.

Game play: The first player picks up a hoop and passes it over his or her body to player 2. Player 2 passes it to player 3, and so on. As soon as player 1 removes the first hoop, the second hoop is started down the line. The goal is to move all of the hoops to the other end of the line.

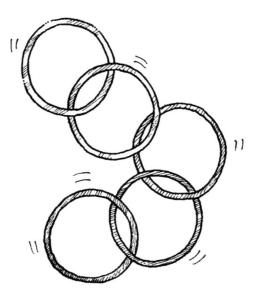

134. HOOPSCOTCH

Grades 2–6

Introduction: This variation on hopscotch is a good station activity.

Equipment:

- 8 hoops per group

Game preparation: Arrange hoops as shown in the diagram. Group players into teams of two and have them stand behind each other, hands on hips or shoulders, and facing hoops 1 and 2.

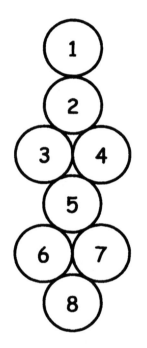

Game play: Each team must jump together, through the hoop arrangement, as in traditional hopscotch landing with all feet in hoop 1, jump and land with all feet in hoop 2, jump and land with each student having one foot in hoop 3 and one foot in hoop 4. They need all feet in hoop 5. Each student needs one foot in hoops 6 and 7. They need all feet in hoop 8 and they need to turn around on one jump in hoop 8 and return to hoop 1 in the same fashion. The team's feet must land correctly in each hoop.

When they miss a jump they need to stop and start over.

135. INVERSION

Introduction: Here's an interesting challenge for a group of 15 to 18 players.

Equipment:

- chalk or string, to make lines

Game preparation: Arrange lines as shown in the diagram. There are two parallel lines 18 inches apart, which are just long enough to fit the group between them. A 20-foot x 18-inch wide area is about right for a group of 16 to 18 players. Line up the students and number off.

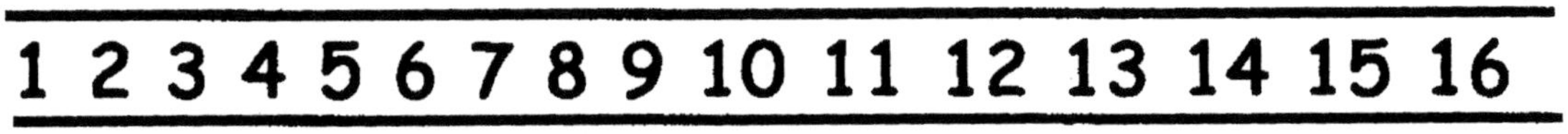

1 2 3 4 5 6 7 8 9 10 11 12 13 14 15 16

Game play: At the signal, the players must reverse their order without stepping outside those two parallel lines. They can crawl under each other's legs or shimmy past each other. If a player steps or falls outside of the lines, the team starts over from the beginning. Let them do it once for practice and then have the group try to set a record.

Tip:

- The game can be made more difficult by making the width between the lines narrower.

136. JET PROPULSION

Introduction: This partner activity is a nice change of pace because the flight path of the balloon is very unpredictable.

Equipment:

- 1 balloon per player
- a finish line

Game preparation: Pair up students and give everyone a balloon (don't share balloons).

Game play: On "go," the first player blows up a balloon and lets it go. The second partner runs to the spot where it lands and does the same with his or her own balloon. Repeat this sequence until one team has crossed the finish line.

137. MACHINES

Introduction: Create a human machine!

Equipment:

- a hat full of machine names on slips of paper (such as lawn mower, garden tiller, typewriter, blender, oil well, washing machine, street sweeper)

Game preparation: Create groups of eight and ask each group to draw the name of a machine.

Game play: The team's task is to use all its members to make the machine come to life. Each team will show off its new machine to the other groups, who try to guess what it is. All members of the group must be involved in the presentation.

When the players demonstrate their machine, there should be no talking. Appropriate sound affects are allowed.

138. MOVING-CIRCLE BALL TOSS

Grades 2–6

Introduction: The goal should be to see how many balls a group of players can keep in the air while running in a circle. This is a good station activity, but it can be exhausting and can also cause dizziness.

Equipment:

- 6 or 7 (8-1/2-inch) rubber balls per group of 8 players.

Game preparation: Arrange groups of eight players in circles. Each person should be spaced about two steps apart.

Game play: Players begin by jogging in a circle. One runner tosses a ball over his or her head to the player behind him or her. That player, in turn, tosses the ball over his/her head to the player behind. Continue until the group masters tossing one ball in a circle.

Tip:

- Add additional balls as the group's skill level increases.

139. NUMBER SCRAMBLE

Introduction: Students cooperate to create a giant number using their bodies?

Equipment: None

Game preparation: Divide the class into groups of five to eight players. Each team should select a name for themselves. It will help them to reorganize when the time comes.

Game play: Begin by asking the players to follow a pathway in the play area using a locomotor skill that you've designated. When you call out a number, the teams need to regroup and try to make that number using *all* of their players in one minute.

Give the team five points if they are successful.

Tips:

- The activity is more fun and can be adapted to any age player if you make them compute the answer, by asking, a question such as "5 + 2 = what?" or "How many points do you score for a touchdown?"

140. OVER THE WALL

Introduction: Set the stage by making up a story about how crossing this wall is important, dangerous, and requires cooperation. Let the players discover the pitfalls on their own. This works well as a station activity.

Equipment:

- high bar
- crash mat
- tumbling mat

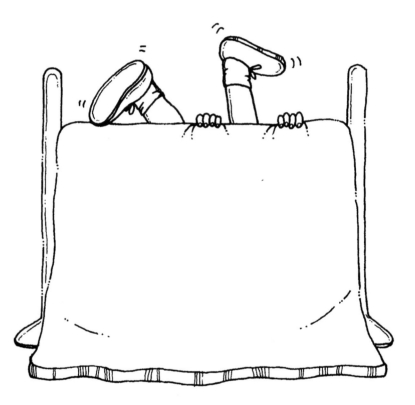

Game preparation: Drape a mat over the high bar. The wall should be higher than the students heads. Place a crash mat below the bar and adjust the height of the bar for the players participating. Keep the bar high enough that it is a challenge to get everyone to the other side. Create groups of five to seven players.

Game play: The group needs to move everyone to the other side of the wall. Players can help only from one side of the mat and they cannot change sides once they are over the wall.

141. PARACHUTE RACE TRACK

Grades 4–6

Introduction: Parachute activities are a great way to promote cooperation by an entire class. It is fun and exciting for the class to keep trying to improve upon its record of successful laps.

Equipment:

- 1 large parachute (25 to 30 feet in diameter)
- 1 ball (8 to 10 inches in diameter)

Game preparation: Space the entire class evenly around the parachute. Ask the players to grip the parachute with two hands.

Game play: Ask the group to see how many times it can roll a ball around the outside of the parachute. Every time the ball goes around the center hole it counts as one lap. The players raise and lower the parachute to propel the ball and are not allowed to touch the ball with their hands. Let the class discover the movements necessary to make the ball roll around the outside of the parachute.

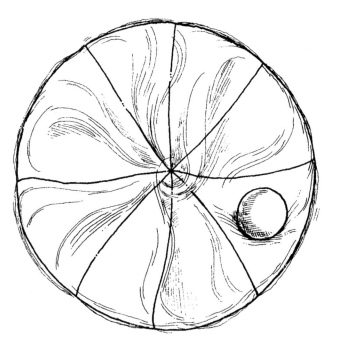

142. PARTNER SCOOTER BASKETBALL

Grades 2–6

Introduction: This unusual variation of basketball requires students to coordinate their actions: one person is in charge of moving around the court, and the other is in charge of handling the ball.

Equipment:

- 1 scooter per every two players
- 2 garbage cans
- 1 rubber ball

Game preparation: Create two teams of equal size.

Game play: This game is played like Scooter Basketball in Section 10 except that the player on the scooter is pushed by a partner. The player riding may never help to propel the scooter, and the player pushing may never touch the ball

143. PIT STOP

Introduction: Complete with a full tank of gas, new tires, and a fresh driver, a human car is pushed by its driver around the racetrack and back to the pit area. A pit crew is standing by to provide assistance!

Equipment:

- enough cones to make one oval track
- a scooter board, pair of coveralls, paper cup, and pair of large shoes per team
- a green flag
- a bucket of water

Game preparation: Create teams of five and designate one team member to be the car and another to be the driver. The other team members are the pit crew.

Game play: At the sight of the green flag, the driver puts on the coveralls while the "car" sits on the scooter board. One crew member fills up the car with gas by giving the car a paper cup full of water. The two remaining crew members change the tires (shoes). The car may not help in any way. And only the pit crew is allowed to touch the cup of water.

When the car arrives back to the pit area, the driver takes the coveralls off and gives them to one of the pit crew. A different crew member gases up the car and the remaining crew members change the tires. To change the tires, the crew person puts the car's real shoes back on the car. When all of the tasks have been completed, the new driver pushes the car around the track.

While the car is racing around the track, one pit crew member needs to get some gas. Every time the car completes a lap, everyone rotates positions, except the car. Continue this pattern until all team members have had an opportunity to play the role of every position on the team.

Rotation of Positions:

1. Driver rotates to left tire changer
2. Left tire changer goes to right tire changer
3. Right tire changer becomes the gas attendant
4. The gas attendant becomes the new driver

144. RADIOACTIVITY

Introduction: The challenge of this small group activity is to move a plastic pail, which represents a uranium isotope, from one circle to another.

Equipment:

- a deflated bicycle inner tube
- 4 (8-foot to 10-foot) jump ropes tied to the inner tube
- plastic pail per group
- chalk

Game preparation: For each group, draw two concentric circles with the chalk. Tie the four jump ropes to the inner tube as indicated in the diagram. Create groups of four players.

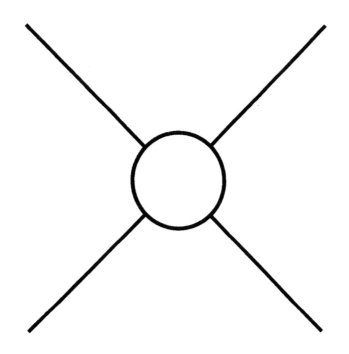

Game play: Each player hangs on to one rope and must stay outside the larger circle. If the players work together, they can pull their ropes in such a way as to make the tube section into a pattern tight enough to slip over the pail and lift it. Their goal is to move the pail (uranium isotope) from one circle to another.

Tip:

- Another option is for two people to pull the inner tube tightly enough to lift the pail. The group then needs to move the pail a certain distance. If they drop the pail, replace it in the circle and start over.

145. ROWBOAT

Introduction: Rowing a boat is a classic team activity—see if you can graduate to crew team!

Equipment: None

Game preparation: Partners sit on the floor, facing the same direction, one behind the other, as if in a rowboat. The back player places his or her legs around the body of the player in front.

Game play: To move, both players lift their bodies up with their hands and arms and move backwards. The front person may use both feet and hands, but the person in the back can only use his or her hands. This motion resembles a pull with the oars. As players master the skill with two people, add more players to the group.

146. SHARKS

Introduction: This is a great activity if you want to work on group process and group cooperation. Begin with an elaborate anticipatory story describing that each group has been shipwrecked on a deserted island. It is temporarily safe but has no fresh water or food. The challenge is to get to a safe area before dark.

Equipment:

- 1 scooter
- 20- to 25-foot long rope
- one mat per team
- chalk

Game preparation: Create teams of five to seven players. Draw a group of rectangles, as shown in the diagram. The large rectangle represents the playing area and is the shark-infested sea. The rectangles in the middle represent islands in the sea.

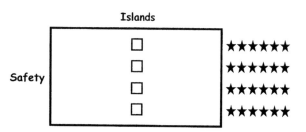

Game play: Each team has a one-person dinghy (the scooter) and a length of rope. In the distance, they can see a small island and they know that on the other side of the small island is "safety." The team members must devise a plan to get one person at a time over to the small island, and return the boat for another team member to use. Remind players not to stand on the scooters. Other than that, they can use the rope and scooter as they wish.

Any time a player touches any body part, even a little finger, in the shark-infested water, that person is devoured by a shark. (These are huge sharks.) The player must perform a "body reward" and then re-enter the game at the starting point. A body reward could be a constructive act such as an opportunity to practice pull ups for 30 seconds on the high bar. This is not presented as punishment but rather as part of the healing process.

If a player falls off his or her scooter in the shark-infested sea, the player leaves to do the body reward but the scooter stays where it landed. It is part of the game for the players to figure out how to get their dinghy back. If they loose their rope, it stays where it landed.

Play until all teams can get to the safe land or for a preset time. Do not help the players with ideas. Enforce the rules strictly and make the players figure out how to save themselves.

Tips:

- Make the island smaller so it limits the number of players that can be on the island at a time.
- Give each player a card that has a number on it. The number designates how much that player weighs. Now the island has a weight limit.

147. SHOE SHOPPING RELAY

Introduction: This combination relay race combined with a shoe hunt makes an exciting field day activity.

Equipment: None

Game preparation: Have everyone take off their shoes and put them in a big pile at one end of the room. Then mix up the pile. Divide the class into teams of four or five players each and organize into lines as in the diagram.

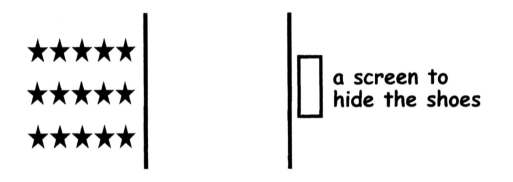

Game play: On the signal "go," the first player in line describes his or her shoes to the second player in line, who runs to the pile of shoes, finds the shoes, and puts them on the first person. If the wrong shoes are retrieved, that player must return them and get another pair. The game continues with player number two describing his/her shoes to player number three. Player number three describes his/her shoes to player number four etc. The last person in line describes his or her shoes to the first person. The challenge is to see how quickly each team can complete the task.

148. SILLY CIRCLE

Introduction: This getting-to-know-you game uses creativity and silliness to break the ice. It works best with older students.

Equipment: None

Game preparation: Ask everyone to form one large circle.

Game play: One player starts the game by moving to the center of the circle using some kind of silly walk. Upon reaching the center, the leader needs to use their name in a short rhythmical phrase which can be accompanied with body motions. (It is best if the name phrase tells something special about the person.) Example: "My name is Jerry! Jumpin' Jerry!" This phrase could be accompanied by a slow straddle jump on the first sentence and two quick straddle cross jumps on the second sentence. Then the leader returns to the edge of the circle using the same silly walk. The entire group now repeats the action and the name phrase with the leader.

The person to the right of the leader repeats the process using his or her own name and new movements.

149. SPACE STATIONS

Introduction: This activity has also been known as Vanishing Hoops.

Equipment:

- several hoops
- CD player

Game preparation: Put out several hoops to represent space stations. The players are referred to as astronauts floating through space. They float while some light music is played. When the music stops, the astronauts are given five seconds to find the nearest space station. If a person cannot find a space station in five seconds or if two astronauts collide in space, they sit out one round.

As the astronauts get better at locating space stations, remove some stations. This is when the game becomes exciting because the game is not limited to having one astronaut per space station. The objective is to just be in a hoop in five seconds. Sometimes six, seven, or more students may all be in one hoop. How many students can you fit in one hoop?

150. SPELLER

Introduction: Play this game with the whole class. Make letters by writing on a large piece of construction paper.

Equipment:

- a cardboard or paper letter of the alphabet for each player
- whistle

Game preparation: Pin a large letter of the alphabet on every player. Avoid the uncommon letters of Q, X, and Z.

Game play: Students begin by following a pathway in the play space. When the whistle is blown, shout a number, for instance, three. Students search for other players with whom they could make a three-letter word. Any players who are unable to become a part of a three-letter word within a reasonable amount of time are given points. A group of three that cannot make a word also earn points. The objective is not to accumulate points.

151.   SQUEEZE BALL WALK

Grades K–6

Introduction: Squeeze ball is an activity that can be done quickly, without any preparation. It can be done as partners or in small groups.

Equipment:

- cage ball or other large ball

Game preparation: Organize the group in a circle. Place the ball in the middle of the circle and have the group hold the cage ball with their bodies. The group cannot use their hands on the ball. This includes getting it off the floor.

Game play: Players must keep the ball in the circle with pressure from their bodies and never allow the ball to touch the ground. The group needs to move the ball from one end of the gym to the other. If it is a mature group, have the group move over, under, or through obstacles.

152. STEPPING STONES TO SAFETY

Grades K–4

Introduction: The goal of this game is for each group to move its team members safely across an alligator-infested swamp.

Equipment:

- 3 carpet squares per group

Game preparation: Designate a line on each side of the gym. Create groups of five or six players and have all of the teams stand behind one line.

Game play: Explain to the players that they need to use the carpet squares as stepping stones to cross the swamp. They can share a stepping stone. They can pick up the stepping stones and pass them from one to another, but they cannot throw them across the floor or scoot on them like ice skates. If someone touches the floor in the alligator-infested water, that person must go to a designated area, perform a body reward, such as a push up, and then rejoin the team at the starting point.

153. SWING IN

Introduction: The object of this game is to see how many people can swing into the same hoop. It is ideal for small groups.

Equipment:

- 1 climbing rope
- 1 hoop
- 1 sturdy table

Game preparation: Place the table beneath the climbing rope and set a hoop several feet away from the table. Line up groups of five or six players behind the table.

Game play: The first player mounts the table, swings on the rope, and attempts to land in a hoop placed away from the table. If that player lands in the hoop, he or she stays there. When the next player takes a turn, the person who is already in the hoop can help him or her land in the hoop. If someone falls out of the hoop or does not make it to the hoop, the whole group must return to the starting point. The group keeps track of its best score and keeps trying to improve upon it.

154. SWITCH AND SWAP

Introduction: The objective is for all the players on one side of a line to switch places with players on the other side.

Equipment:

- 1 carpet square per player and one extra

Game preparation: Place the carpet squares in a line about 18 inches apart. Create two teams of about five or six players, and have them line up on the carpet squares. There should be one empty square between the facing teams.

$$\boxed{6}\ \boxed{5}\ \boxed{4}\ \boxed{3}\ \boxed{2}\ \boxed{1}\ \boxed{0}\ \boxed{1}\ \boxed{2}\ \boxed{3}\ \boxed{4}\ \boxed{5}\ \boxed{6}$$

Game play: Players may move forward into the free spot or jump over an occupied space to a free space. Only one player is allowed to occupy a space at a time. If the team can successfully trade places, everybody wins.

155. ZOOM

Introduction: This game is played in one large group. Along with being entertaining, this game is a good way to help players learn what a group "personal record" is.

Equipment: None

Game preparation: Have all players form a circle with their shoulders touching. Designate a player to be the group leader.

Game play: The group leader turns to the player to his or her right and says "zoom." That player turns to his or her right and says "zoom," and so on. Time the group to see how long it takes "zoom" to travel completely around the circle. Once you call the time, the group leader starts a new turn. The group's goal is to beat their previous record.

Tips:

- As an added challenge, have players to the right and left of the group leader say zoom and pass it on, so that two turns around the circle are completed simultaneously.

- Try sending other sounds, gestures, or objects around the circle (a clap, a hand squeeze, a ball, or a bowling pin, for example).

Section 9

GAMES INVOLVING STRIKING SKILLS AND EYE-HAND COORDINATION

One of the goals of physical education is to teach lifelong skills and appreciation of sports to children. Some of the most popular sports in our culture involve the use of racquets—tennis, racquetball, pickleball. and badminton, for example. For students to participate in games using racquets, they need to develop eye-hand coordination skills.

At the elementary level, you can teach eye-hand coordination to students through several movement experiences that involve racquets, paddles, and other types of novelty equipment.

Because gymnasium space is limited, it is sometimes difficult to offer the students opportunities to use these skills in game situations. This section provides some games that enhance striking skills and other forms of eye-hand coordination without requiring as much space as regulation net games.

156. BALLOON-MINTON

Grades 3–6

Introduction: This game is the same as badminton, except it is played with a balloon instead of a shuttlecock.

Equipment:

- badminton racquet for each player
- balloons
- badminton net
- badminton court (smaller court also suitable)

Game preparation: None

Game play: Play this game exactly like traditional badminton; however, allow children two hits to get the balloon over the net and move the serving line closer to the net.

Tips:

- Because the balloon will not move as far as a shuttlecock, you can reduce the size of the court; however, the net should be left at regulation height.
- Use high quality latex balloons. Not only will they last longer, but because they are slightly heavier, they are easier to hit over the net.

157. SIDEWALK TENNIS

Grades 4–6

Introduction: Sidewalk Tennis gets its name from the origin of the game: tennis played on the sidewalk.

Equipment:

- paddles
- net (optional)
- 1 tennis ball (or nerf ball)

Game preparation: If a regular sidewalk is being used for the court, use four squares. If marking courts in the gymnasium, follow the directions shown in the diagram; the game is played by two players. Designate one to be the server and one the receiver.

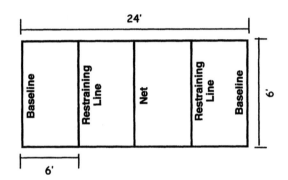

Game play: The server, standing behind the baseline, bounces the ball and serves with an underhand hit over the net or net line. The ball must land in the opponent's court. The receiver may hit the ball after it bounces once. After the receiver has returned the serve, the players may return the ball either while it is still in the air or after it has bounced once. However, balls that land in front of the restraining line must bounce before they can be returned.

Only the server scores points. He or she continues serving until a side-out is scored. Points are scored similar to volleyball.

The following plays constitute fouls:

Hitting a serve before it bounces

Hitting a ball in front of the restraining line before it bounces

Server steps over the base line on the serve

Serving the ball with a side or overhand stroke

Tips:

- Games are usually played to eleven or fifteen points. If the score is tied at ten or fourteen points, a player must make two consecutive points to win the game.
- To play doubles, the same rules apply, but with partners alternating on serves and returns. When a player loses a serve, it goes to an opponent.

158. SMALL BALL TETHERBALL

Grades 3–6

Introduction: This game is just like traditional Tetherball, except it is played with paddles and a small ball in place of the large rubber Tetherball.

Equipment:

- Tetherball assembly-rope
- two wooden paddles
- one ball (a small plastic Whiffle ball attached to the rope works well)

Game preparation: Use a regular Tetherball layout. Randomly select the first server and opponent. The two stand on opposite sides of the pole, facing each other.

Game play: The server starts the game by serving the ball—tossing it into the air and hitting it with the paddle—in either direction. The ball must go around the pole once with no one hitting it. When the ball goes by the opponent the second time, he or she may hit it, but in the opposite direction. The players continue to hit the ball back and forth with their paddles, each one trying to wrap the rope around the pole. The player who succeeds in doing this is the winner. The game can also be won by the player whose opponent commits one of the following fouls:

- Hitting the ball with any part of the body instead of with the paddle
- Touching the pole
- Hitting the rope with the paddle

Tips:

- If only two people are playing at a time, the winner of a game is the server of the next game. When one player wins four games, the set is over.
- If there are players waiting in line, a faster method of rotation needs to be employed; traditionally the winner of the preceding game stays, becomes the server and a new challenger enters the game.

159. QUOIT TENNIS

Grades 4–6

Introduction: Quoit Tennis does not involve striking skills, but it does reinforce eye-hand coordination and throwing skills, which are related to striking skills.

Equipment:

- 1 net

- one quoit

Game preparation: The size of the playing court can vary depending on the number of players. A volleyball court can be used for teams of six to nine players per team, a badminton court could be used for teams of two to four players per team, or smaller court sizes could be used for doubles or singles. The net should be about five feet high and there should be a line on each side about three feet away from the net to mark "no man's land."

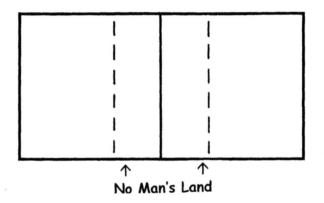

No Man's Land

Game play: The game begins with a serve, which takes place from behind the serving team's back boundary line. The serve is executed with an underhand or sidearm toss and must go over the net.

The receiving team must catch the quoit in the air (a rule can be made to either catch with one hand or two hands. The player catching the quoit may only take one step before throwing the quoit back over the net. Players must not step out of the boundaries of the playing court or step into "No Man's Land" for any reason.

If a quoit lands in "no man's land" it does not count as a point for the team that served or threw it; the opposing team simply picks up the quoit, moves out of "no man's land," and continues the rally.

Tips:

- The game is scored the same way as volleyball. Points can be scored only when a team is in control of the serve and forces the opposing team to commit an error. Games are played to fifteen points.

- Regulation games are supposed to be played to 15 points, but good shorter games can be played to 7 or 11 points.

160. CATCH BALL

Introduction: This cooperative game works well as a station or as a partner challenge activity.

Equipment:

- one catch ball for every two players (a catch ball looks like a giant jack with numbered spokes)

Game preparation: Group players in pairs. Have players in each pair stand about twenty feet apart. (Modify the distance based on players' skill level.) Give a catch ball to one player in each pair.

Game play: The player with the catch ball tosses it to the other player, who must catch it with one hand. The team scores points according to the number on the spike the player grabbed to catch the ball. The team keeps adding up the scores for each successful catch made during an assigned time limit.

Tips:

- Younger children should be allowed to catch with two hands, but designate which hand will be used for determining the points the team will be awarded.

- As the players get better at this game, add the following bonus rule: As the thrower releases the catch ball, he or she calls out the color of one of the spokes. If the catcher can catch the ball on that color the team doubles the points for that catch.

161. FLING IT

Introduction: Sometimes called a mono-fling, this game can either be played cooperatively with a partner or competitively. It also works well as a station activity.

Equipment:

- one "Fling It" per player (A "Fling It" is a net about 12" by 24" with handles on each end.)
- one "Fling It" ball per couple

Game preparation: Players stand about twenty feet apart.

Game play: Players must fling the ball back and forth to each other by cradling it in the net and propelling it forward by "flinging it" out of the net. Players can play cooperatively, seeing how many successful passes they can make, or play competitively over a net with boundaries and try to score points. This game can be scored the same as volleyball.

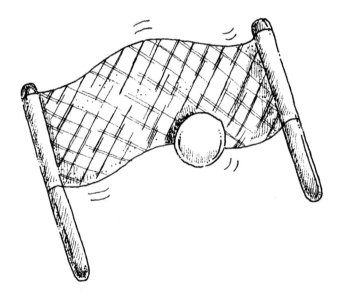

162. FOXTAILS

Introduction: This game works well as a station activity or as a challenge played individually or in teams of two.

Equipment:

- one foxtail per game (a foxtail is a ball with a long tail of three different colored stripes sewn to it)

Game preparation: Players stand thirty feet or more apart.

Game play: As players throw the foxtail back and forth, their objective is to catch the foxtail by the tail—and the farther away from the ball the better. Scoring is tallied as follows: if players catch the foxtail by the bottom third of the tail (the part farthest away from the ball), they get five points; they get three points for grabbing the middle part of the tail; and one point for grabbing the part of the tail closest to the ball. (The three parts of the tail are distinguished by color.) Catching the ball itself scores no points.

The two players play for a designated time to see how many points they can accumulate together.

163. VOLLEYBIRD

Grades 4–6

Introduction: This game is popular in South America. It can be played either competitively or cooperatively.

Equipment:

- one volleybird (A volleybird looks like a giant badminton birdie.)

- a net

Game preparation: Set up a 5'-high net at mid-court. (The height of the net can be adjusted depending on the players' skill level. Designate court boundaries to suit the skill level of the players.

Game play: Play this game according to the rules for volleyball. If playing one on one, a player needs to return the Volleybird on every hit. If playing two on two, three hits are allowed per side, as in volleyball.

Tips:

- This is a great game for developing skills with both the left and right arms.

- If you're using this game as a station activity, have the players see how many hits they can get in succession. (This is a good way to use the activity with younger children.)

- The game can be played one on one or two on two.

Section 10

MAXIMIZING PARTICIPATION IN TEAM SPORTS

In the physical education curriculum, it is difficult to offer students equal feelings of success when playing team sports. Students who are less skilled in a specific activity may be discouraged by their inability to keep up with their more skilled peers. Many traditional team sports are highly competitive games that were originally designed for play by adults, yet children who lack the physical or emotional mastery to participate in these activities are often required to do just that in physical education programs. And just because all those players are on the field or court, it doesn't necessarily mean they are all participating. Often, a minority of more skilled or aggressive players dominates the game.

The objective of this section is to provide experiences similar to those of the major team sports such as basketball, soccer, and baseball, but with one major difference: the games featured here have far less emphasis on winning, and much more emphasis on maximized participation and enjoyment for all players. These games and activities will also provide students with an opportunity to refine the skills such as throwing, kicking, and catching that are prerequisites for many team sports. Most of the games here are variations on ones which children are already familiar. The games are organized according to the similarities of the skills used in each game.

164. ALASKAN BASEBALL

Introduction: Alaskan Baseball is a simplified version of baseball.

Equipment:

- 1 soft volleyball

Game preparation: Divide players into two equal teams. One team scatters in the field to play defense and the other team plays offense. Using a traditional baseball field layout, the offensive team lines up behind home base.

Game play: Using a volleyball serve, the first player on the offensive team hits the ball into the field. The server then runs around his or her teammates who are standing in line behind home base. The team gets a point for each circle the batter completes.

The player who fields the ball must stand where the ball was fielded. All of the defensive players must then run and line up behind the player who fielded the ball. Defensive players must pass the ball through their legs, making sure that every player handles the ball. When the last player has the ball, that person yells "Stop," at which time the batter stops running around his or her teammates. After every batter on the offensive team has batted, the teams trade places.

165. BASEBALL VOCABULARY GAME

Grades 4–6

Introduction: This written challenge will help children become better acquainted—in a humorous way—with baseball and softball lingo.

Equipment:

- 1 worksheet and pencil per student or per team

Game preparation: Give each student or team a worksheet and a pencil.

Game play: Students must match the terms in the right-hand column to the terms in the left-hand column. To use this as a game, give players a designated time period to complete the worksheet. The player or team with the most right answers at the end of the time period is the winner.

Baseball Vocabulary Worksheet

_____ 1. A summer pest   **a.** plate

_____ 2. A famous Greek poet   **b.** mask

_____ 3. Inaccurate   **c.** catcher

_____ 4. Unmarried   **d.** curve

_____ 5. A successful effort   **e.** double·

_____ 6. Used for pancakes   **f.** single

_____ 7. Vessel for pouring   **g.** fan

_____ 8. A good foundation   **h.** fly

_____ 9. To take unlawfully   **i.** error

_____ 10. A brief visit   **j.** hit

_____ 11. A dinner necessity   **k.** pitcher

_____ 12. If you forget your door key   **l.** steal

_____ 13. A disguise   **m.** short stop

_____ 14. Used to gain relief in hot weather   **n.** base

_____ 15. Proprietor of dog pound   **o.** out

_____ 16. A coveted jewel   **p.** diamond

_____ 17. Dangerous on highways   **q.** sacrifice

_____ 18. An offering   **r.** bat

_____ 19. To multiply by two   **s.** homer

_____ 20. It only flies at night   **t.** batter

Answers: 1-h; 2-s; 3-i; 4-f; 5-j; 6-t; 7-k; 8-n; 9-l; 10-m; 11-a; 12-o; 13-b; 14-g; 15-c; 16-p; 17-d; 18-q; 19-e; 20-r

166. BRAUNBOLL

Grades 4–6

Introduction: This game comes from Finland and is similar to softball. The differences are that in Braunboll there is an increased level of participation and decreased risk of failure for all players. Also, in this game the defense earns most of the points.

Equipment:

- several items to use for bats (plastic bats [for indoor use], regular bats [for outdoor use], and basic wooden paddles)
- gloves (optional)
- balls (for outdoor play, use restricted-flight balls; for indoor play, use plastic Whiffle ball)
- home plate for the batter and a base for the catcher
- four cones for the bases

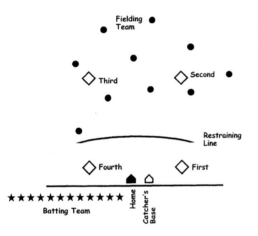

Game preparation: The play area should be set up as shown in the following diagram. Players on the batting (offensive) team should all be lined up behind home plate.

Game play: Hitting: Each batter may choose any item to use as a bat, but must use the same bat for his/her entire turn. Batting is done fungo style and players have two chances to hit the ball. The batter must hit the ball past the restraining line and within the first base and fourth base lines for the ball to be in play. If a player fails to hit the ball or get an in-bounds hit on two attempts, the defense gets one point, and the player still gets to go to first base (cone). The hitting team gets one point every time a player makes it to home base.

Fielding or defense: Fielders should scatter in the field but may not position themselves any closer to the batter than the restraining line. The fielders field every ball and throw it to the catcher. When the catcher catches the ball, he or she steps on the catcher's base and shouts "Braun." At that point, every base runner freezes. The defense receives one point for every runner caught off base. Runners caught off base return to the last base they touched safely. If a runner has not returned to a base before the next hit, the defense gets a point. When a fielder catches a fly ball, the defensive team receives three points; however, the batter and base runners advance as if it was a normally hit ball. The fielding team still needs to return the ball to the catcher to stop the play and the advance of the base runners.

Base running: Base runners may advance any number of bases on any hit. They do not need to run to the next base unless they feel they can make it safely. There can be any number of runners on a base and they may advance in any order. Base runners return to the batting line in the order which they finish running the four bases. It isn't necessary for runners to touch the bases (cones). They just run close to the cone.

Innings: Each team bats for a designated length of time (typically between three and five minutes). At the end of that time, the teams change places. Because the batting order changes as players run the bases, the batting order is not fixed and is determined by how players line up when they come in from the field.

Point Summary: Batting team—one point every time a base runner makes it to home base. **Fielding team**—one point each time a batter fails to hit the ball on two strikes or to hit the ball past the restraining line and between first base and fourth base, one point each time a batter fails to hit the ball or get an in-bounds hit (past the restraining line and between first base and fourth base) on two attempts, one point for every base runner caught off base when the catcher shouts "Braun," three points for catching a fly ball.

167. DANISH ROUNDERS

Grades 3–6

Introduction: Here is a modified version of Danish Rounders.

Equipment:

- soft volleyball
- 4 bases

Game preparation: Arrange the bases and the players as shown in the diagram. The fielding team may not take positions closer than the restraining line. When possible, take the role of catcher for both teams. If this is inconvenient, a player from each team can take the catcher's position for the team.

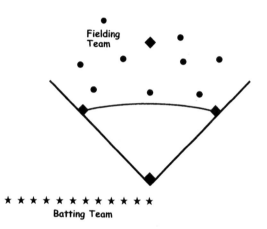

Game play: The action starts with the catcher (teacher) standing to the side of the batter, tossing the ball about 2 feet above the batter's head and straight up above home plate. Using his or her hand, the batter must hit the ball into the field before it hits the ground. Each batter gets three chances to hit the ball before making an out.

The fielding team must return every batted ball to the catcher who must then down the ball (bounce the ball on home plate and then catch it). If the ball is downed before the runner reaches a base, the runner is out.

Any number of base runners may be on a base at the same time. Players only run when they feel they can make it to the next base safely. Whenever the ball is downed by the catcher, a base runner who is not on base is out. A caught fly ball is an out for the batter. All other runners must tag up before advancing to the next base. The batting team gets one point for every player reaching home safely.

Play is continued until all members on the batting team have been put out and then the two teams change sides. When a player is put out they leave the game. The players scoring runs get back into the batting line. The batting team continues to bat until all of the batting team has been put out or runners are stranded on base and there are no more batters to hit them in.

Another option is to switch sides after a designated number of outs, such as five, has been made.

168. ICEBERG

Introduction: Like other games featured in this section, this game involves hitting and fielding a ball with maximum participation for all players.

Equipment:

- 1 volleyball or soccer ball
- 4 bases

Game preparation: Use a basic softball field for this game. The fielding team scatters in the field and the batting team lines up in a single file line behind home base.

Game play: Batters can hit the ball into the field by kicking it, hitting it with their hands, by using a paddle, etc. The first person in line, the batter, hits the ball into the field. Following the batter, the batting team runs single file around the bases. The team earns one point for every person touching home base.

The fielding team must throw or pass the ball to every player on the team, throwing it to the pitcher last. Fielders can get into any formation to do this. When the pitcher receives the ball, he or she yells "Iceberg," at which point all runners freeze. (The runners touch all of the bases as they run, but being on or off a base is irrelevant at this point.) The runners stay where they were frozen. The next batter leaves their spot and goes up to bat. When the ball is hit all of the frozen runners resume running the bases, staying in the single file line. All players bat in order. When a runner reaches home base he or she starts running to first base again.

The whole team bats before changing sides or to keep the game moving at a faster pace, switch sides after five batters have hit the ball.

169.   KICK-BASKET-BALL

Grades 4–6

Introduction: This high-energy game is a combination of kickball and basketball. Players kick, throw, catch, and shoot baskets.

Equipment:

- 2 (8 1/2- or 10-inch) rubber utility balls
- 4 portable bases or poly spots
- 1 regulation basketball basket

Game preparation: Lay out the playing field as in the diagram. The offensive team lines up behind the basket. The first player in line on the offensive team is the kicker; the second player in line is the thrower and holds the second ball. The fielding team spreads out on the field as in baseball, with one player being the pitcher, and one being the team shooter.

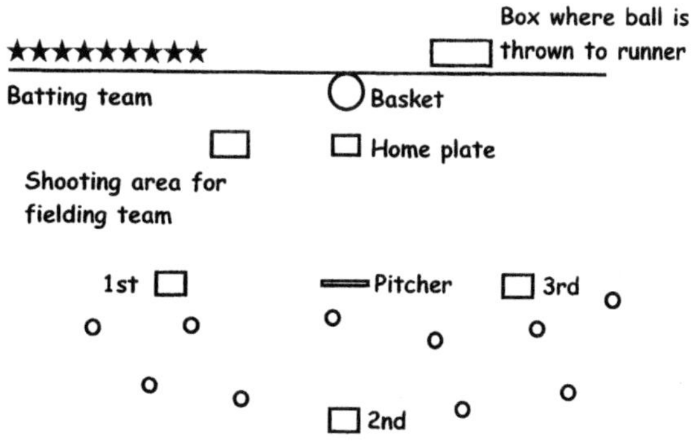

Game play: Play begins with the pitcher rolling the ball to the kicker. The kicker kicks the ball and has to run all four bases. The thrower for the offensive team can throw the ball to the base runner (the kicker) after he or she has rounded third base. To complete a turn the runner must make a basket, taking as many shots as needed to make one. After the base runner (the kicker) makes a basket, he or she runs home. The thrower then becomes the next kicker, and the next person in line becomes the thrower. Meanwhile, players on the fielding team must retrieve the kicked ball and throw it to first base, second base, and third base. The third baseman throws the ball to the designated team shooter, who shoots a basket, taking as many shots as needed to make one. If the kicking team scores a basket first, the team gets a point. If the fielding team makes a basket first, it is an out against the kicking team. At the start of each player's turn, the pitcher gets one ball and the offensive team's thrower gets the other.

Teams can switch places either after a designated number of outs or after every player on the kicking team has had a turn.

Tips:

- The fielding team could rotate defensive positions after each batter to allow every player to play different positions.

195

170. BALLOON BLOWER BASKETBALL

Grades 4–6

Introduction: Here's a novel spin on the game of basketball in which the action is constant.

Equipment:

- 1 basketball per team
- balloons

Game preparation: Teams of four or five players line up behind their designated baskets and shooting lines. Each team chooses one player to be the balloon blower. Assuming in a gym, using real basketball baskets.

Game play: On the start signal, players in each line take turns shooting baskets. Shooters must rebound their own shots and return the ball to the next shooter. Each time a player makes a basket, that team's balloon blower may take one long blow on the balloon. The first team to pop its balloon wins.

171. BASKETBALL 21 (THREE SHOT)

Grades 4–6

Introduction: This game is a variation of the traditional game of 21. It works well either as a station or played with several small teams.

Equipment:

- 1 basketball per team
- 1 basket per team

Game preparation: Organize players into small teams (three to five players per team). Teams line up behind their designated baskets and shooting lines.

Game play: On the start signal, the first player from each team takes a long shot from the shooting line. The shooter scores three points if this shot is made. The player then takes a second shot from wherever he or she recovers the ball. A basket on this shot is worth two points. On the third shot, the player dribbles to the basket, shoots a lay-up, and scores one point if the shot is made. The first player now goes to the back of the line and the next player repeats the process.

Play continues until either one team reaches a designated winning score, or until a designated time period ends.

172. BASKETBALL ROB THE COOKIE JAR

Grades 3–6

Introduction: This is the same game as Rob the Cookie Jar (see page 103), except now players must dribble a basketball when they run to get a cookie.

Equipment:

- 16 bean bags

- 5 hoops and one basketball per team

Game preparation: Arrange five hoops (cookie jars) as shown in the diagram. Place the bean bags (cookies) in the center cookie jar. Divide players into four teams and have each team form a line behind their own cookie jar.

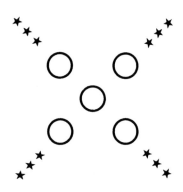

Game play: Each team's goal is to store a cache of six cookies. When you give the start signal, the first person on each team dribbles to the cookie jar to steal a cookie. After stealing a cookie, players go to the back of their team's line. Players keep taking cookies from the jar until it is empty, at which point players can steal cookies from each other's cookie jars. Because no team can defend the cookies in its jar, there is always a place from which to steal a cookie. The player going after a cookie must always dribble the basketball. If a player loses control of the dribble, he or she must go back to the team without a cookie. If the player has already stolen a cookie, the cookie must be returned to the cookie jar from which it was stolen. The first team to have six cookies in its cookie jar wins.

Tips:

- Teach players that strategy is important to winning in this game, because not only should they be working to get six cookies, but they should also try to take the cookies away from teams who are close to winning.

- If the game gets too easy, reduce the number of cookies available in the game or increase the number of cookies that a team must get to win.

- Make sure that only one player from a team is stealing at one time. It is easy for the players to get excited and grab cookies out of turn.

173. FAST PASS

Introduction: This game reinforces basketball passing and interception skills.

Equipment:

- identification vests for one team
- 1 basketball

Game preparation: Divide players into two teams of 4 to 5 players per team, and have players from one of the teams wear identification vests. Designate a play area of approximately 30' x 30'.

Game play: At the start signal, the team with the ball (randomly chosen) must try to complete five consecutive passes without the ball being intercepted by the defensive team. The defensive team attempts to intercept the ball or recover an incomplete pass, but may not foul an offensive player. Every time a pass is completed, the team shouts the number of the pass completed. If the pass is intercepted, the new team with the ball starts the count over at number one. A team that completes five passes gets one point and starts the pass count over at number one.

174. BASKETBALL VOCABULARY GAME

Grades 4–6

Introduction: This challenge will help children become better acquainted—through a fun written activity—with basketball lingo.

Equipment:

- 1 worksheet and pencil per player or team

Game preparation: Give each student or team a worksheet and a pencil.

Game play: Students must match the terms in the right-hand column to the terms in the left-hand column. To use this as a game, give players a designated time period to complete the worksheet. The player or team with the most right answers at the end of the time period is the winner.

Basketball Vocabulary Worksheet

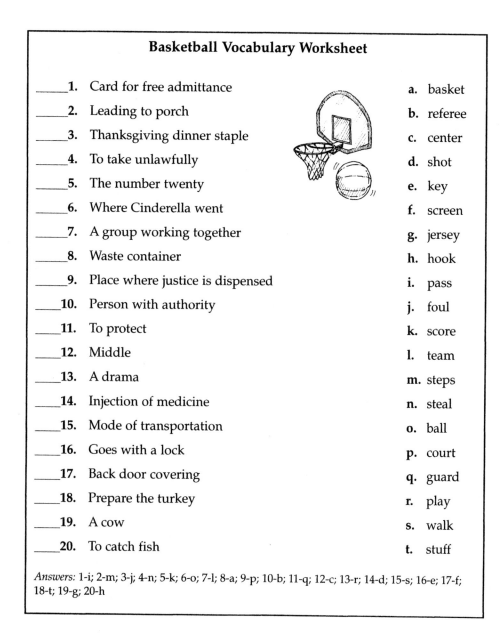

_____	1.	Card for free admittance	a.	basket
_____	2.	Leading to porch	b.	referee
_____	3.	Thanksgiving dinner staple	c.	center
_____	4.	To take unlawfully	d.	shot
_____	5.	The number twenty	e.	key
_____	6.	Where Cinderella went	f.	screen
_____	7.	A group working together	g.	jersey
_____	8.	Waste container	h.	hook
_____	9.	Place where justice is dispensed	i.	pass
_____	10.	Person with authority	j.	foul
_____	11.	To protect	k.	score
_____	12.	Middle	l.	team
_____	13.	A drama	m.	steps
_____	14.	Injection of medicine	n.	steal
_____	15.	Mode of transportation	o.	ball
_____	16.	Goes with a lock	p.	court
_____	17.	Back door covering	q.	guard
_____	18.	Prepare the turkey	r.	play
_____	19.	A cow	s.	walk
_____	20.	To catch fish	t.	stuff

Answers: 1-i; 2-m; 3-j; 4-n; 5-k; 6-o; 7-l; 8-a; 9-p; 10-b; 11-q; 12-c; 13-r; 14-d; 15-s; 16-e; 17-f; 18-t; 19-g; 20-h

175. SCOOTER BASKETBALL

Grades 4–6

Introduction: Scooter Basketball is a novel and challenging variation on the game of basketball.

Equipment:

- 10 scooters
- 2 large rubber ball or basketball
- identification vests for half of the players or one team
- 2 garbage cans
- 2 tumbling mats

Game preparation: Divide the class into two equal teams. Have one team wear identification vests. Teams stand on sidelines opposite each other. Five players from each team go to the middle of the court and sit on scooters next to an opponent whom they will guard when their team is on defense. A player's bottom must always be on the scooter. Place baskets on tumbling mats on opposite ends of the court.

Game play: Start the game with a jump ball at mid court. Play using the rules for basketball, but without dribbling and with the following modifications.

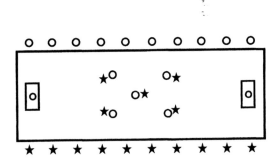

Players may move the ball by either carrying it, passing it to a sideline player (sideline players may not shoot baskets), passing it to another player on a scooter, or shooting a basket.

- If a player falls off a scooter while he or she has the ball, that player must immediately put the ball on the floor and get back on the scooter. The ball is a free ball while it is on the floor and any other player may grab it. Players cannot roll onto the mat, thus preventing anyone from getting too close to the basket.

- After a basket has been scored, the referee takes the ball out of the can and awards it to the other team's sideline. Play continues from there.

After a designated time limit or score has been reached have teammates switch positions, with players on the scooters going to the sidelines, and the next five players on the sidelines taking the scooters.

Tips:

- Add dribbling to the game just as in real basketball.

176. ALLEY HOCKEY

Introduction: This game will help students learn to play positions and enhance their hockey skills.

Equipment:

- enough cones to mark the alleys
- floor hockey equipment for each player

Game preparation: Set up a playing area as for floor hockey. Use cones to designate alleys. Divide players into two teams.

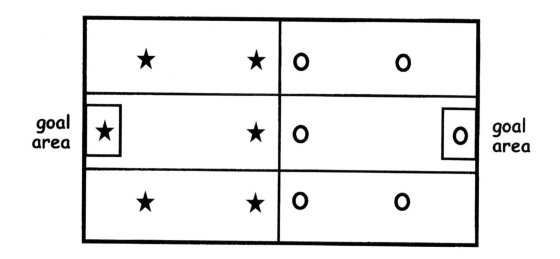

Game play: Play this game according to regulation floor hockey rules, with the exception of having players stay in their alleys at all times. After each score or at a designated time rotate positions.

Tips:

- Remind the wings or offensive players to play on the offensive half of the field, the defenders to play the defensive half of the field, and the centers to play the middle part of the field.

177.   GRAB-A-FLAG

Introduction: This is a great game for practicing flag pulling for flag football.

Equipment:

- 2 flags per player

Game preparation: Players take scattered positions throughout the playing area. Players "wear" their flags by holding them in place with their belts or by wearing flagbelts.

Game play: On the start signal, players begin running and stealing as many flags as possible, while trying not to lose their own flags. At the end of a set time (one or two minutes) the players stop and count their flags. The player with the most flags wins.

Tips:

- To have more than one winner, declare all players with more than two flags as winners.
- Try a variation of this game called Share the Flag, in which players who lose both flags are frozen, and players with more than two flags can unfreeze them by giving them a flag.

178. KICK OFF

Introduction: This is a good game to introduce players to the kick off procedures in a flag football game.

Equipment:

- identification vests for one team
- 1 football
- 1 kicking tee
- flags for each player

Game preparation: Mark a playing area approximately 50 feet wide and 100 feet long. Divide players into two teams (referred to here as the red team and the green team) and give one team identification vests. Divide each team into groups A and B. Have the teams line up as shown in the diagram. The red team's group A players are the receivers—the offense—and the green team's group A players are the kickers—the defense. Each team's group B lines up on the sideline.

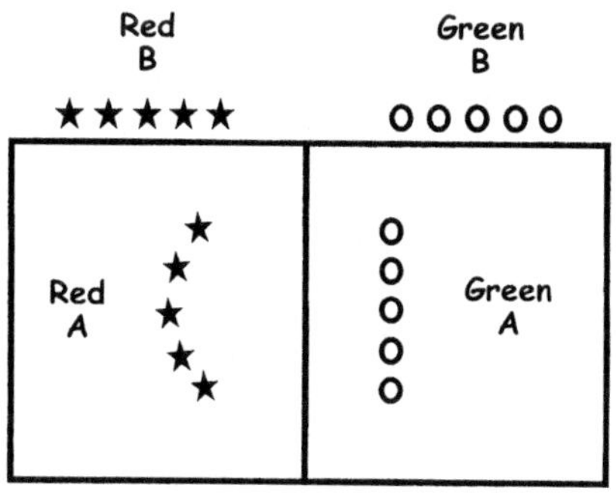

```
        Red              Green
         B                 B
     ★ ★ ★ ★ ★         O O O O O
   ┌──────────────┬──────────────┐
   │              │              │
   │         ★    │   O          │
   │        ★     │   O          │
   │  Red   ★     │   O   Green  │
   │   A          │   O    A     │
   │        ★     │   O          │
   │         ★    │              │
   └──────────────┴──────────────┘
```

Game play: The green team kicks off. A player on the red team catches the ball and runs to make a touchdown. The play stops when the ball carrier's flag is pulled or a touchdown is scored. The offensive players are encouraged to run interference for the ball carrier. A touchdown is worth 6 points.

Groups A and B on each team now rotate positions as follows: Players on the sidelines move into the play area, on the same side (kicking or receiving) they're on. Players who were in the kicking or receiving group go to the sidelines on the opposite side from the one they were on (e.g., from receiving area to kicking sidelines). Based on the diagram above, this would work as follows: green A goes to the sidelines at the receiving end of the field; green B now becomes the new kicking team; red A moves to the sidelines at the kicking end of the field; and red B becomes the new receiving team. This rotational process is followed at the end of each play. The waiting teams should get ready quickly so the game will move along rapidly. Even though there are four groups the score is kept as the red team and the green team.

179. ALLEY SOCCER

Introduction: This game will help players learn to play positions as well as enhance their soccer skills.

Equipment:

- enough cones to mark the alleys
- 1 soccer ball
- identification vests for one team

Game preparation: Set up a playing area as for soccer. Use cones to designate alleys. Divide players into two teams and have one team wear identification vests.

★	★	O	★	★	O
★	★	O	★	★	O
★	★	O	★	★	O
★	★	O	★	★	O

Game play: Play according to regulation soccer rules, with the exception of having players stay in their alleys at all times. The game progresses as a normal game of soccer. A goal is scored when one team kicks the ball below head level over any part of the goal line. After each score, rotate positions.

Tips:

- Encourage the forwards to play at the offensive end of the field, the halfbacks to play the center half of the field, and the fullbacks to play the defensive part of the field.

180. MULTIPLE GOAL SOCCER

Grades 4–6

Introduction: This game is based on regulation soccer, but with a major variation.

Equipment:

- 4 soccer goals
- identification vests for at least one team
- 2 soccer balls

Game preparation: Mark off a square (not rectangular) soccer field, with side boundaries between 50 and 60 yards long.

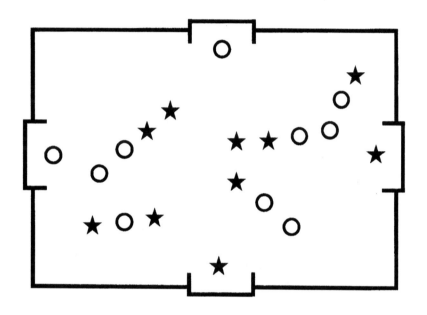

Game play: Follow regulation soccer rules, but with the following changes. Set a goal in the middle of each sideline. Each team defends two goals on facing sides of the field, and is allowed a goalie for each. Play with two balls at the same time.

To start the game, give a ball to two opposing goalies. The goalies put the balls into play with goal kicks. When a goal is scored, the ball is put back into play with a goal kick at the goal where the score was made. The team with the most goals at the end of a designated time wins.

Tips:

- Encourage teams to play positions as in regular soccer, as this will improve their offensive and defensive play.

181. PIN DOWN

Introduction: This fast-paced game will help players practice the skills needed to defend a soccer goal.

Equipment:

- 16 bowling pins
- 4 to 8 sponge Nerf® balls

Game preparation: Arrange the bowling pins in a grid, in an area about 40 feet wide and 40 feet long. Assign one player to defend or protect each pin. The remaining players line up on one of the sidelines in single file formation, as indicated in the diagram.

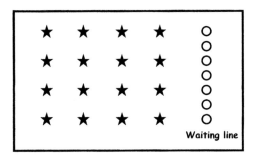

Game play: Randomly give out four balls to players in the play area. The players guarding the pins in the playing area attempt to knock down the other players' pins. Players may leave their pins to chase balls or to dribble a ball toward another player's pin and shoot at it. Players may not use their hands to defend their pins.

When a player's pin is knocked down, that player yells "pin down" and leaves the playing area and goes to the end of the waiting line, and the first player in the waiting line enters the game. The new player sets up the downed pin and is ready to play.

Tips:

- Increase the number of balls in play as players' understanding of the game increases. The more balls being used, the faster the waiting line moves.

182. TIGHTWAD BALL

Grades 2–6

Introduction: This is an excellent activity for teaching the dribbling skills used in soccer, basketball, and floor hockey.

Equipment:

- a ball for all but 3 to 5 players

Game preparation: Select three players to be "it." The "its" do not receive a ball. All other players receive a ball and scatter in the playing area. Specify the dribbling skill to be used—for example, soccer, basketball, etc.

Game play: On the start signal, all players begin dribbling and moving in all directions in the playing area. At the same time, the "its" begin trying to steal a ball. The "its" may not foul a player while trying to steal a ball. When a player's ball is stolen that player becomes the "it" and immediately begins trying to steal a ball from someone.

183. BALLOON VOLLEYBALL

Grades 3–6

Introduction: This variation on volleyball can be used as a station activity or a small group game.

Equipment:

- at least 1 (10-inch to 14-inch) balloon for every game
- portable nets

Game preparation: Set up a net about 6 to 8 feet wide and 4 to 5 feet high. Group players into teams of two, and have one team take a position on each side of the net.

Game play: Play according to regulation volleyball rules and require that players only use legal bumps and sets. (If the players are allowed to tap the balloon with their fingers, the game won't be very exciting.) Serves must be made from about three steps from the net and must make it over the net. After the serve, teams can use three hits to get the balloon over the net. Players should be encouraged to use bump, set, and spike on every rally.

184. FOUR SQUARE VOLLEYBALL

Grades 5–6

Introduction: This game is similar to the traditional playground game of four-square and allows for teams of two to three players.

Equipment:

- volleyball nets
- 4 standards
- 1 trainer volleyball or beach ball

Game preparation: Crisscross two volleyball nets and number the courts as shown in the diagram. Organize players into teams of two or three, and assign one team to each court. Extra teams line up behind court 1. Score and errors are the same as in traditional volleyball.

Game play: The ball is put into play with a serve by a player from court 4. The serve must be made from behind the end line of that team and may go to any of the other three courts.

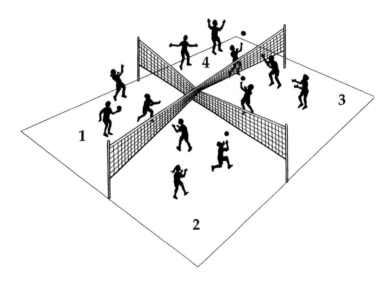

After the serve, play follows regular volleyball rules. The ball may be played into any court. A team commits an error by failing to return the ball to another court within the prescribed three volleys or by causing the ball to go out of bounds.

A team that commits an error leaves the court and goes to the end of the waiting line behind court 1. All of the remaining teams on the court move up one court—e.g., from court 1 to court 2, court 2 to court 3, etc.—as that is the court the new team entering the game will take.

Court 4 is the most desirable and a team's chief objective is to stay in court 4 as long as possible. If a team in court 4 maintains court 4 for two or more serves in a row, the players must rotate servers for every serve.

185. BUKA

Introduction: The official name of this game is Sepak Takraw. It is extremely popular in Thailand, Malaysia, and other Southeast Asian countries.

Equipment:

- 1 Buka ball per game

- a net

- net standards

Game preparation: Set up a badminton-sized court with a 5-foot high net. Set up the court as shown in the diagram. Divide players into teams of three. Select a serving team and a receiving team to start the game. The serving team's forwards stand in their quarter circles, while the serving back must have only one foot in the serving circle. The receiving team's players may stand anywhere in their side of the court. Players can move freely on each half of the court once the ball has been served.

Game play: The game begins when one of the serving team's forwards tosses the Buka to the serving back. The back must then kick the ball with the foot that is outside the serving circle into the opponents' court in one try. The serve is good even if it hits the net before going into the other half of the court. A team is allowed three hits to return the Buka ball. The same player may make all three hits.

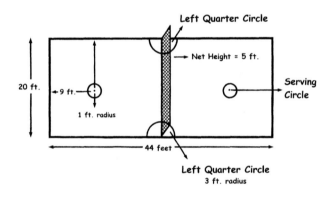

As in volleyball, only the serving team can score. The first team to score fifteen points wins. The game follows basic volleyball play with the additional errors.

The following count as errors:

- The back does not kick the ball over the net on the serve

- The ball falls to the ground inside or outside of the court

- The ball is hit more than three times in succession by one side

- The ball hits the net but does not go over it

- The ball hits a player's hand or arm

- Any part of the body touches, crosses the plane, or goes under the net

- The ball rolls on a player's body or is stalled

Section 11

PLAY DAY ACTIVITIES

The tradition of having a Play Day or Field Day at the end of the school year is a very popular one. Such events give students the opportunity to participate in some friendly contests with their classmates just for the fun of it.

All the games presented in this book so far have been for a purpose—that is, to help students develop a physical education skill. As a result, not too many relay races have been included, as they are not always success oriented or developmentally appropriate activities for a physical education class. Therefore, this section is devoted solely to games that are fun but may not necessarily have a learning objective. The goal of these activities is to get everyone involved in laughing, having fun, and sometimes even in getting wet. These activities are not recommended for physical education class.

There are hundreds of basic activities that can be used for a Play Day or Field Day, and I'm sure that as a physical educator, you are well aware of the traditional activities. This chapter will focus on activities that are a little out of the ordinary. While these activities may take some additional preparation, the final outcome is worth the extra effort.

In addition to the activities suggested here, you may also want to consider some of the activities found in the Cooperative Games section (pages 131–176) for your school's Play Day. The concepts of equality, participation, success and trust discussed in that section can be applied to Play Day activities to enhance the experience for all the participants.

The activities in this section are listed in alphabetical order and each activity has a recommended grade level. However, you are the best judge of which of these games will work for the participants in your school's Play Day.

186. NO-HANDS BALL CARRY

Introduction: This is a cooperative activity in which participants need to have a little patience with their partners.

Equipment:

- short strips of rags for tying the participants hands behind their backs
- 1 large playground ball per team

Game preparation: Players form teams of two, and all players must have their hands tied behind their backs. Partners stand facing each other with a ball on the ground between them. Designate a start line and a finish line 25 to 30 feet apart.

Game play: At the start signal, players on each team must work together to try to get their ball off the ground and carry it to the finish line. If the ball drops, (they are both carrying it) either player on the team may retrieve it and kick it back to the spot where it was dropped. The players can again try to pick up the ball and try to reach the finish line. There is no limit to the number of drops a team can make. The first team to get its ball to the finish line wins.

Tip:

- Try this activity using larger balls or with more players per team.

187. BALLOON SWEEP

Introduction: This basic relay race is best performed indoors. If played outdoors, a very still day is best as the wind could be a major factor.

Equipment:

- 1 broom or hockey stick for each team
- 1 balloon for each team

Game preparation: Designate a starting line and a goal line about 30 to 40 feet apart. Place a cone on the goal line in front of each team. Divide the players into three teams (3 to 4 players per team).

Game play: On the "go" signal, the first player on each team begins to sweep the balloon toward, around their goal, and back to their team. Each player does the same task in turn. The winning team is the team finishing first. Even if a team is behind, they should not give up because many unexpected things may happen, as the balloons do not always go where the sweeper thinks they will go.

Tips:

- To make it more difficult, a small obstacle course could be set up for each team to sweep their balloon through.
- Extra balloons should be readily available to replace broken balloons.

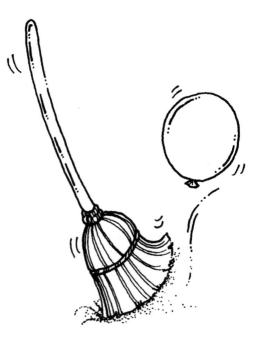

188. BOTTLE FILL

Introduction: Here is a fun-filled relay race that will provide many laughs (along with damp clothes).

Equipment:

- several small paper cups
- 1 plastic soda bottle and a bucket of water per team

Game preparation: Divide players into teams of five or six players. Designate a start line and a finish line (about 50 feet apart). One player from each team goes to the goal line, lies down on his or her back, and holds a soda bottle on his or her forehead. The remaining players from each team all line up at the start line.

Game play: On the start signal, a player from each team scoops up a cup full of water and runs to the person holding the bottle and tries to fill the bottle. After pouring the water into the bottle (or on the player on the ground), each player must run back to his or her group and hand-off the cup, at which point the next player repeats the process. Play continues until one team has filled its bottle and is declared the winner, or until a designated time is up, in which case the team with the most water in its bottle wins.

Tip:

- Have good-humored players hold the bottles because they will get wet!

189. BREAD AND WATER RELAY

Grades 4–6

Introduction: Eating and drinking was never as difficult as it is in this race.

Equipment:

- a half piece of bread and 1 small cup full of water per player
- 2 small tables per team (cardboard boxes turned upside down work well as tables)

Game preparation: Arrange the course layout as shown in the diagram. Have teams line up in file formation behind the starting line.

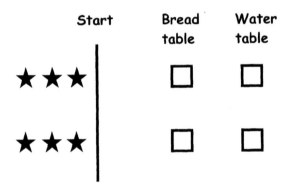

Game play: On the start signal the first player from each team runs to the first table and eats one piece of bread. Players may not leave the table until the entire piece of bread is in their mouth. From the first table, players run to the next table where they must drink an entire glass of water. Again, they may not leave the table until the glass of water has been drunk. Once players have completed this task, they run back to their team and tag the next player who must perform the same procedure. This continues until all of the players from one team have successfully completed these tasks. The first team to accomplish this is declared the winner.

Tips:

- Add more eating stations but make sure whatever needs to be eaten is in small pieces and soft. Sticky foods like taffy would not be good choices. Also avoid foods that pose allergic-reaction risks.
- Have one helper available to fill water glasses and lay out the new pieces of bread.

190. EXTREME EGG AND SPOON RACE

Grades 4–6

Introduction: This is a traditional relay race, but in this version, participants must hold the spoon—by its handle—in their mouth and place their hands behind their backs.

Equipment:

- 1 plastic spoon for each person
- hard boiled eggs to carry in the spoon(peanuts, walnuts, or marbles are good substitutes to use for eggs)

Game preparation: Divide players into teams of 5 or 6 players. Designate a start line and a finish line (about 50 feet apart). Give each player a spoon, then have team members line up at the start line.

Game play: On the start signal, the first player from each team must carry the egg on the spoon to the finish line and back. The only time players are allowed to use their hands is to pick up the egg and put it back on the spoon. As each player completes this task, the next player in line for that team must also perform the task. This continues until all of the players from one team have successfully completed carrying their egg to the finish line and back. The first team to accomplish this is declared the winner.

Tips:

- Although you may think of this activity as geared toward younger players, carrying the spoon in your mouth can make this very humorous for older children to try to balance the spoon and egg as they try to make it to the finish line and back.

191.   FAN THE BALLOON RELAY

Introduction: This event is based on the basic relay format. It is best played indoors because the outside air will blow the balloons off track.

Equipment:

- 1 or 2 pieces of cardboard for fans and one balloon per team

Game preparation: Divide players into teams of 5 or 6 players. Designate a start line and a finish line (about 15 feet apart). Give each team a balloon and a cardboard fan, then have team members line up at the start line.

Game play: On the start signal the first person in each team tosses up a balloon and tries to make it to the finish line and back while keeping the balloon afloat by fanning the air under it. When the first player on the team returns, the second player should start by taking the fan from the first player and not allowing the balloon to touch the floor or stopping the balloon with his or her hands. This continues until all players have had a turn.

Tips:

- Have two people from the same team, each with a fan, go at the same time. Use this variation especially if one person cannot keep the balloon up.

- Use a large balloon and have the whole team work together to move the balloon a desired distance and back to the starting spot.

192.   FOUR LEGGED RACE

Introduction: This activity takes the old three legged race and expands it to be a more cooperative and skillful activity.

Equipment:

- rubber strips cut from car inner tubes to hold players' legs together (flag belts also work well)

Game preparation: Group players into teams of three. Strap the inside legs of the outside people to the legs of the middle person. Designate a starting line and a finish line (about 40 feet apart).

Game play: On the start signal, each team of three players must try to reach the finish line without falling. The first team to make it is the winner.

Tips:

- It's best if participants have practiced and learned to move and fall together prior to racing as a team.
- Instead of declaring only one winner, you could use a success-oriented approach in which all of the groups that finish without falling receive a first-place award, groups that finish with only one fall receive a second-place award, and so forth.

193. JELLO SLOUPH

Introduction: This contest takes some preparation; however, it's well worth the effort because it's sure to be a hit.

Equipment:

- 1 small square of Jello placed in a paper cupcake holder per person
- 1 table (or cardboard box) on which each team's Jello can be placed

Game preparation: Teams of 4 to 6 players are lined up in traditional relay style, with each team facing the table where the team's Jello squares are placed.

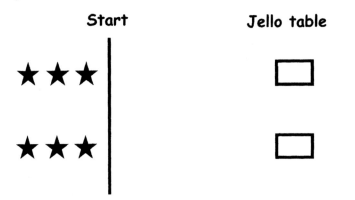

Game play: On the start signal, the first player from each team runs to the team's table, and with hands behind his or her back, attempts to "slouph" (eat) the Jello. A player may not return to the team until he or she has eaten all of the Jello in the cupcake holder. A team is finished when all of the team members have eaten their Jello.

Tips:

- A judge should be at each table to determine that the Jello has been eaten and to make sure the other pieces of Jello do not get accidentally spilled.
- This is an excellent activity for a special teachers' race at the end of the Play Day.
- Your school's kitchen staff may be willing to make the Jello. If not, ask for parent volunteers to provide Jello cut into little squares and placed in cupcake holders.

194. GRAND PRIX

Introduction: This event tests players' ability to give and take directions. The students will enjoy this challenge and the laughs that come with it.

Equipment:

- 6 to 8 cones
- 1 scooter
- 1 stopwatch
- blindfolds for half of the players

Game preparation: Divide players into teams of two—a rider and a driver. The person on the scooter is the rider and gives the directions. The person pushing is blindfolded and is the driver. Lay out a simple course as shown in the diagram. Each team takes a turn on the course.

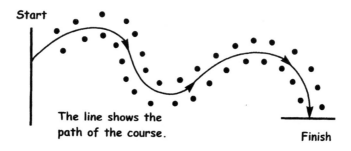

Game play: The rider sits cross-legged on the scooter, hanging on to the scooter with two hands. The rider may never manually help steer the scooter. The driver, who is blindfolded, places his or her hands on the rider's shoulders. On the start signal, the rider begins giving directions for the driver to follow to get through the obstacle course. Use a stopwatch to time each team, and record the times. The team that is able to get through the course in the shortest time is the winner.

Tips:

- Consider giving penalty points for hitting cones, if the rider falls off the scooter, or if the rider helps the blindfolded driver steer the scooter.

195.   I'VE GOT MY HANDS FULL
Grades 1–6

Introduction: We all know how frustrating it is when we have our hands full of stuff and have to find a way to carry one more thing. That is the experience players will have in this challenging relay.

Equipment:

- identical sets of items for each team (brooms, balls, bathroom tissue, boxes, etc.; choose items that are easier to carry for the younger students; for the older students choose items that are awkward to carry)

Game preparation: Organize players into teams of four. Teams must line up in traditional relay style facing a table about 30 feet away. Place all of each team's items on the table in front of the team.

Game play: On the start signal, the first player in each team runs to the table, picks up one item, runs back to the team, and gives it to the next player. The second player carries the first item, runs back to the table, picks up another item, returns to the team and gives both items to the third player. (No items are ever put back on the table.) Each succeeding player carries the items collected by their teammates to the table, picks up one new item and carries them all back to the next player. The first team to successfully transport all the items from the table back to the starting line is the winner.

Once picked up, an item cannot touch the table or floor. Any item dropped in transit or transfer must be returned to the table. No one may assist the giving and receiving players in their exchange, except through coaching. If there are 12 items each player will make at least 3 trips before they finish.

Tips:

- Teams should take some time to plan their strategy. For example, a good strategy would be to keep the objects that are harder to carry for last.

196. I'M NOT THIRSTY RACE

Grades 1–6

Introduction: Play Days usually make everyone thirsty; this race allows participants to get a drink as part of the action.

Equipment:

- 1 small paper cup for each person
- 1 bottle of drinking water per team.

Game preparation: Group players into teams of four to six players. Teams must line up in traditional relay style facing a finish line about 30 feet away. Place a large, clean container of cool water for each team directly opposite the team on the finish line.

Game play: On the start signal, the first player in each team runs to the team's water container, pours a cup of water, drinks it, returns to the team and tags the next player, who then does the same thing. This continues until the container is empty or a designated time period has expired. The team finishing all of its water first—or the team that drank the most water in the designated time period—is the winner.

Tips:

- Make sure the container of water will allow for at least three cups of water per player.
- It may be a good idea to have a judge at each water station to make sure players are drinking their water and not spilling more than the occasional drop or two.

197. LE MANS TUG OF WAR

Grades 4–6

Introduction: This activity combines the elements of a short foot race with traditional tug of war.

Equipment:

- 1 good tug of war rope

Game preparation: Set up the tug of war rope as for a regular tug of war event. Mark a starting line parallel to the rope, about 25 feet away. Have the players from each team take starting positions on opposite sides of the starting line.

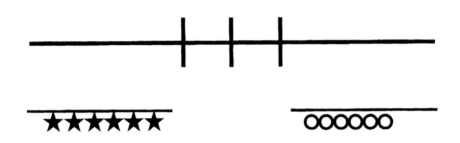

Game play: On the start signal, the teams race to the tug of war rope, grab it, and start pulling. Basic tug of war rules apply after the pulling starts.

Tips:

- A little practice ahead of time makes this game even more fun.
- Best performed in a grassy area in case of slips or falls.

198. READY, AIM, FIRE!

Grades 3–6

Introduction: The suspense in this activity helps build the excitement.

Equipment:

- enough water pistols for half of the group

- music CDs and CD player

Game preparation: Fill half of the water pistols. Line the group up in two concentric circles, partners facing each other. Give players in the inner circle water pistols and have them hold their hands behind their backs. Players holding the water pistols must always keep them behind their back.

Game play: As game play begins, each circle must rotate one-quarter turn to the players' right. When you start the music , both circles walk straight ahead in their line of direction. (There are now two groups walking in opposite directions.) When you stop the music, the students in both circles face their new partners. The students in the outer circle close their eyes. The game leader says, "Ready, Aim, Fire!" On the word "Fire," all of the inside-circle players shoot at their partners. (All players switch circles). After each turn, players in the inner circle pass their guns around the circle (so as not to give away who is holding a water-filled gun) and the whole process is repeated again.

Tips:

- Secure permission from the school administration to use water pistols at school prior to Play Day. If using water pistols at school is a problem, try using small plastic squeeze bottles to squirt water.

- Players should have the opportunity to be in both circles several times.

- This is an especially great activity on hot days.

199. WATER BALLOON NEWCOMBE
Grades 4–6

Introduction: This game provides plenty of excitement as players throw water balloons back and forth over a volleyball net. This game follows the rules of Newcombe.

Equipment:

- plenty of water balloons
- a volleyball net

Game preparation: Set up a play area and teams just as for volleyball.

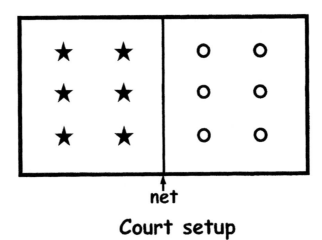

Court setup

Game play: Newcombe is played following the rules for volleyball, but instead of striking the ball, players throw and catch it. A player who catches the ball can either throw it back over the net or throw it to a teammate closer to the net for a shorter throw over the net. A team can make three passes on its side of the net before throwing the ball over the net. After catching the ball, a player is only allowed one step in which to throw it. In this variation of Newcombe, players are catching and throwing a water balloon instead of a ball. A team scores a point whenever the opposing team breaks a water balloon. The object of the game is not to break the water balloons.

Tip:

- If players are highly skilled try playing the game with two water balloons at one time.

200. WATER BALLOON ON THE HEAD

Grades 3–6

Introduction: The wetter players get in this event, the higher the team's score will be.

Equipment:

- 15 to 20 water balloons per team

Game preparation: Designate a breaking line and a starting line about 30 feet apart. Have players for each team take their positions as shown in the diagram, with player 1 at the breaking line, and the remaining players lined up in single file behind the starting line. Each team's water balloons should be placed near the team at the starting line.

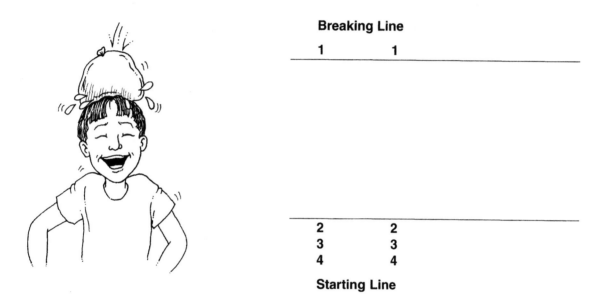

Game play: On the signal "go," player 2 picks up a water balloon and runs to the player on the breaking line. Player 2 throws the balloon into the air, at least 3 feet above player 1's head. Player 1 must try to get into position to break the water balloon by ramming it with his or her head.

Player 2 now takes player 1's place on the breaking line and player 1 returns to the back of the line behind the starting line. This continues for a specified time limit (one or two minutes) with all players taking their turn in order. Each team gets one point for each balloon that touches a breaker's head but does not break and five points for each balloon that is broken on a teammate's head.

Tips:

- Have plenty of towels handy for players when game play has finished.
- Discuss any safety concerns to the students before beginning game play; have participants bring dry clothing to change into after game has been played.

201. MISCELLANEOUS PLAY DAY ACTIVITIES

Grades K–6

The following are some very traditional activities that have been used at Play Day events for years and that are always a hit with Play Day participants. The titles are self-explanatory.

- Jump Rope for Speed (for thirty seconds, one minute, etc.)
- Rope Climb for Speed
- All sorts of short sprint type races (for example, 30-yard dash, 50-yard dash, etc.)
- Scooter races of all types
- Marble and Spoon Race
- Shoe Scramble
- Three–Legged Race
- Shoe Kick
- Sack Races
- Frisbee Throw Activities
- Suitcase Relay
- Balloon Squash
- Balloon Stomp
- Water Balloon Toss
- Tug of War

INDEX
(alphabetical by game)